The TURKEY HUNTERS

THE LORE, LEGACY AND ALLURE OF AMERICAN TURKEY HUNTING

EDITED BY

BRIAN LOVETT

PHOTOGRAPHY BY

TES RANDLE JOLLY

(UNLESS OTHERWISE INDICATED)

Published by

krause publications
An F&W Publications Company

700 East State Street • Iola, WI 54990-0001
715-445-2214 • 888-457-2873
www.krause.com

Our toll-free number to place an order or obtain a free catalog is 800-258-0929.

Library of Congress Catalog Number: 2003108896
ISBN: 0-87349-578-0

Styled by Gary Carle
Edited by Joel Marvin

Printed in the United States of America

DEDICATION

To Jennifer, without whom none of this would mean anything.

CONTENTS

FOREWORD

Thanks at least partly to the fact I've been involved with *Turkey & Turkey Hunting* in some capacity from its inception, the magazine holds a special place in my hunter's heart.

Given my deep, abiding interest in the sport's roots, it's somehow appropriate the first article I wrote for the magazine — it appeared in the first issue — was on the literature of turkey hunting. It's some index of the growth of turkey hunting's popularity that in a dozen years since, that the value of most of the books mentioned has at least quadrupled.

Since that first issue — the ensuing years have flown like a spooked gobbler off the roost — I've worn many hats with the magazine, including free-lance contributor, consulting editor, co-editor (with one of the grand old gentlemen of the sporting world, Gerry Blair), and for the past few years, editor-at-large. I take considerable satisfaction in having played at least a modest role in the magazine's evolution. Primarily, that has involved interaction with some first-rate editors and several of the finest, most knowledgeable sporting scribes in the country. You will see sterling examples of their work in these pages, and in my biased opinion, you can search in vain to find better magazine coverage of turkey hunting.

Like me, one of these writers, Lovett Williams, the dean of American wild turkey biologists, has been a constant presence in the magazine from the outset. His insightful words figure prominently here, and they indicate that one constant hallmark of *T&TH* has been to provide readers with in-depth understanding of their quarry.

Similarly, endeavoring to capture the passion turkey hunters hold for the grand bird has always been another aspect of the magazine's thrust. You will find plenty of stories here loaded with a love for the sport. The thoughtful musings of Joe Arnette have reminded us — in every issue — that hunting is only part of it. One of his most telling pieces — they are all good — is reprinted here. In the magazine and these pages, we get pointed — and sometimes painful — reminders of the sport's ethics, plus stories of success and failure.

Turkey hunters love the sport's traditions and lore and also feel a special link to the land. In this book, you will sense and share those considerations in various ways — from the staunch guidance of a hunter's father to the exuberance of a spring camp; from the joys of an exceptional first gobbler to the feelings of loss when urban sprawl consumes a favorite turkey hunting haunt. If you don't get teary-eyed when you read Tes Randle Jolly's "Ashley's Wish," a serious session of self-analysis might be needed. If you don't learn from the wisdom of seasoned hunters such as Michael Hanback, John Trout Jr. and Jim Spencer, maybe you should be reminded of words penned a century ago by Horace Kephart, the dean of American campers: "In the school of the outdoors, there is no graduation day." Rest assured, seasoned hunters such as these fellows have been to the mountain and have a knack for taking you there, too.

Looking through the table of contents also reminded me of two distinctive and significant aspects of my career hunting and writing about turkeys. One focuses on how privileged I've been. Amazingly — a testament to countless marvelously misspent days — I've shared hunts or camps with most of the writers in this book. I've followed in the footsteps of Williams as he closed ground on a lonely bird after a fall flush that would have done the finest American Indian woodsman proud. I've missed a Rio Grande in inglorious fashion with Brian Lovett next to me. I've killed a fine Alabama tom with Tes Randle Jolly and her husband, Ron, a few yards away manning a video camera. (Incidentally, Tes is responsible for most of the striking photography that graces this work.) Spencer and I have swapped lies and tried alibis. I've shared laughs and professional concerns with Laurie Lee Dovey (we've each served as president of the Outdoor Writers Association of America). Roger Hook has gently — in the only way a preacher could — consoled me when misfortune seemed a temporary mistress in Missouri. And no one could ask for a finer hunting buddy than Terry Madewell.

Even those with whom I haven't hunted are friends. In fact, this anthology has only two contributors I don't know personally. As much as anything, that speaks volumes about the close-knit nature of the turkey hunting world. Every spring, there's a sort of national family reunion — a gathering of the clan, if you will — and it's a joy and privilege to be part of that.

Equally revealing are some of the words and phrases you'll encounter in these pages — "The Miracle of Spring, "I Believe," "Your Land Espoused," "The Magnificent Obsession," "No-Name Turkeys" and "What Can Go Wrong Now?"

Our sport is comprised of a glorious mix of misery, marvels, misfortune and magic. It holds our souls in thrall and fills our dreams with wonder. That's true no matter your sex or age, and it's no mistake that several women and more than one seasoned veteran are among the contributors to this book. All of us share one thing: We are hooked; a collection of hopelessly lost addicts who live for spring and never get enough of that heart-rending, soul-searing fix provided by a lusty gobble. That's why I'm so fond of a quote from one of my favorite hunters of yesteryear, Archibald Rutledge: "Some men are mere hunters," he wrote. "Others are turkey hunters."

I'm proud and privileged to belong to the latter group — "the others" — just as I'm proud to have been associated with the magazine that furnishes the basis for this anthology. Lovett did a fine job in his years as editor of *T&TH*, and the passion that drove him in that capacity shines through in this book. It is written by turkey hunters for turkey hunters, and Lovett is a staunch member of our ranks.

He recognizes, like me, that turkey hunting is an intensely personal activity. To be blunt, anyone who takes it casually needs to find something else to do. They do not belong in the breed apart; the dedicated yet in some senses hapless group author Tom Kelly calls The 10th Legion. On the other hand, for those — like Lovett — who have lost a corner of their souls to His Majesty, the wild gobbler, a rare treat awaits.

So sit back, perhaps with a comforting dose of anti-snakebite medicine, and enjoy a full measure of literary pleasure. You'll find plenty here to brighten your turkey hunting days and lighten your armchair ways.

— Jim Casada

INTRODUCTION

My involvement with *Turkey & Turkey Hunting* was a wonderful accident.

Oh, I'd worked on and off with some aspects of the magazine since arriving at Krause Publications in November 1994. But most of that was in a supporting role. After all, my main duties were with *Wisconsin Outdoor Journal*, and *T&TH* was in the capable hands of co-editors Gerry Blair and Jim Casada, plus managing editor Gordy Krahn.

But during Summer 1995 — the exact date escapes me — Gerry informed KP that he would step down from his editor's chair. The company decided to bring the magazine in-house, and Patrick Durkin, my boss at the time, asked if I'd take the reins.

Of course I was excited and dumfounded. I loved turkey hunting, although I was fairly inexperienced, and the chance to work with the magazine was too much to pass up. So began an incredible six-plus-year journey into the world of the wild turkey.

From my first issue — there's not enough time to laugh at the mistakes — through my first "company" hunt with Don Shipp and Cuz Strickland — during which I realized I knew nothing about turkey hunting — until my final issue one cold winter day, it's been the time of my life. The magazine let a wide-eyed 20-something guy from central Wisconsin thrill to gobbling mornings from New York to the Western prairies, and from Minnesota down through Sonora, Mexico. Along the way, I met some of the greatest people in the country — turkey hunters — and saw some of the best gifts God sprinkled on the Earth.

You can imagine that I faced a tough choice during Winter 2002, when I decided to step away from *T&TH* to edit Krause's newest venture, *Bass Pro Shops' Outdoor World* magazine. I did so only after being promised I could still write for and be somewhat associated with *T&TH*.

It wasn't until months later when Don Gulbrandsen, of Krause's Books Division, and I met that *The Turkey Hunters* came up. We had kicked around the idea previously, but, for one reason or another, it had never come to fruition. However, I couldn't resist the chance to compile this book,

which, I thought, would serve as a fitting coda to my tenure with *T&TH*. Besides, it would be way too much fun.

As I started to formulate the concept of the book, I decided to shy away from practical "how-to" stories. They've always been popular with *T&TH* readers, but they didn't seem to fit into my idea for a comprehensive book. Rather, as had been done in the 1997 Krause book *The Deer Hunters*, I decided to explore the history, lore, lure and allure of turkey hunting. I wanted to examine the amazing comeback and appeal of the turkey, and examine the cult-like devotion turkey hunters have for their sport. Further, I wanted to pay tribute to the greatest aspect of turkey hunting: the many bonds and relationships turkey hunters form, whether to the land, each other or other aspects of the activity. Eventually, I divided the book into three sections: "The Grand Bird," which discusses the turkey and many issues facing it; "The Magnificent Obsession," which touches on the fanatical devotion turkey hunters have for the bird; and "The Turkey Hunter's Ties," which focuses on the sport's "etceteras" and relationships.

From there, I reread almost every column and feature that had appeared in *T&TH* during my editorship. Realizing that wasn't enough — I didn't want the book to merely be a "best-of" compilation from my years at *T&TH* — I read many more from before my time, and even lifted some great turkey stuff from other Krause publications. The package was honed and fine-tuned with some original pieces, and everything came together with the foreword from Casada and the outstanding photography from Tes Randle Jolly.

I was pleased with the final product. It was a labor of love, so I fretted incessantly about what to include and what I couldn't fit in. I hope you'll agree that it tries to capture the heart of one of the most noble, enjoyable and addicting activities imaginable — one I've been involved with for years, thanks to that wonderful accident.

So here it is. I hope you enjoy and learn from *The Turkey Hunters* for years. After all, it's for — and about — you, the turkey hunter.

— Brian Lovett
March 2003

ACKNOWLEDGMENTS

When I left the editor's chair of *Turkey & Turkey Hunting* in early 2002, I intended to write the farewell column to end all farewell columns. That is, I planned to name and honor every person with whom I'd hunted or shared a camp.

After I was about 200 words into the damned thing, I realized it was futile. There was no way I could name everyone. Hell, I couldn't even list a fraction of the deserving folks.

I fear this will be no different. So, let me apologize in advance and tell you this: If I was fortunate to meet or hunt turkeys with you during my tenure at *Turkey & Turkey Hunting*, I haven't forgotten. In fact, I'll always cherish the memory. So, folks who aren't named here should realize that the omission is solely on this page. Your names, faces and actions are still fresh in my mind.

First, thank you, Mom and Dad, for being such great parents and instilling in me a love for the outdoors. Believe it or not, I was listening all those years ago. And although Dad and I never got a turkey during those early hunts, the time was well-spent.

Thanks also to all the teachers and professors who helped and guided me along the way. Again, I can't name all of you, though you surely deserve it. But I must offer special thanks to Charles Bohage, my high-school history teacher, and many of my college journalism professors, including Gary Coll, Gene Hintz, Peggy Davidson and Jean Matheson.

My early career would have been a much rockier road without patient, skilled folks such as Patrick Durkin, Mike Woods, Dennis Dougherty, Stew Rieckman, Mary Martin and Barbara Benish. Thank you for all the lessons through those years.

Thanks again go to Durkin and Debbie Knauer, who brought me to Krause Publications in November 1994 and saw fit to hand me the *T&TH* duties in August 1995. I hope your trust was not misplaced.

Of course, the magazine had long been successful before I arrived. Credit for that belongs to longtime editors Gerry Blair and Jim Casada, who, issue after issue, gave readers the best turkey hunting magazine in the country. Thanks also to Gordy Krahn, who let me help out with the magazine before my name appeared there.

Blair and Casada would probably agree that the magazine is successful in no small part because of its outstanding staff. I salute Casada, the magazine's editor-at-large, and contributing editors Blair, Michael Hanback, Jim Spencer, Scott Bestul, Lovett E. Williams Jr., Jay Langston and Joe Arnette for outstanding contributions to *T&TH*. Your work is the heart and soul of the magazine.

Of course, many other folks — many whose names appear in this book —contributed to *T&TH* through the years. I can't list you all here, but thanks nonetheless. Your passion and knowledge of the wild turkey are evident in your writing and photography.

Many faces in the Krause Publications family also deserve recognition. Thanks to co-workers Dan Schmidt, Ryan Gilligan, Paul Wait, Joe Shead and Dan Brownell for all your help and hard work. Thanks also to old co-worker Bart Landsverk and former associate editor Dave Beauchaine, who worked many long hours on *T&TH*.

I must give special thanks to longtime managing editor Jennifer West, and *T&TH* and *Outdoor World* designer Al West, who have made these magazines read and look better than I could have ever hoped.

And thanks to Jim Schlender, who now heads up *T&TH*. You're doing a great job with my favorite magazine. Also I can't forget Don Gulbrandsen, who kept the idea for *The Turkey Hunters* fresh for years and worked with me to see it through, or Joel Marvin, who did a fine job editing the book and seeing it through production.

During my time at *T&TH*, I was privileged to share the woods with many of the folks who appear regularly in the magazine. At the risk of being accused of name-dropping, here's to all the well-known hunters who have shared their knowledge and time with me. They include, in somewhat chronological order, Don Shipp, Cuz Strickland, Bob Walker of Alabama, Greg Neumann, Tom Neumann, David Hale, Harold Knight, Steve Stoltz, Mark Drury, Bo Pitman, Gary Sefton, Jerry Peterson, Tad Brown, Pat Reeve, Allen Jenkins, Bob Dixon, Darrel Daigre, Brad Harris, Ray Eye, Bob Walker of Walker's Game Ear, Kyle Hicks, Jim Clay, Tom Duvall, Larry Shockey, Matt Morrett, Brian Pierson, Alex Rutledge, Dick Kirby, Mark and Cathy Scroggins, Ernie Calandrelli, Chris Kirby, Brian Ross, Al Mattox, Dodd Clifton, Michael Waddell, Mike Miller, Ron and Tes Jolly, C.J. Davis, Walter Parrott, Jerry Martin and too many others to list. Special thanks, too, to all the guides, landowners and hunting partners not named here. As I said, you're not forgotten.

Tes Randle Jolly deserves special thanks for her outstanding photography that graces these pages. Tes, your work has made this book shine.

Of course, there would be no *Turkey Hunters* if not for one important group: you, the turkey hunters. Without you, *T&TH* and this book would not exist. Your passion and dedication to the wild turkey are evident. Thanks for your feedback, criticism, support and advice through the years. I've been lucky to chat with many of you and look forward to talking with those of you I haven't yet met.

Last, thank you, Jenny, for your love and support during our marriage. Like I said, without you, none of this would mean anything.

THE
GRAND
BIRD

*E*xamining the foremost aspect of turkey hunting is easy.
It begins and ends with the turkey.

The bird — and, as mentioned later, its gobble — provide the
basis for the American turkey hunting subculture. Without the
turkey and its mesmerizing qualities, everything else would be
moot.

You can hunt throughout the world and never find
a quarry as mystifying, frustrating and ultimately rewarding as
the wild turkey. The activity it spawns demands great
understanding, woodsmanship and special skills. Even after
you've acquired and honed those abilities, a gobbler will still
whip you much more often than not. It's no wonder the bird gets
under your skin.

This section isn't an all-encompassing examination of the
bird's biology, behavior and appeal, though it touches on that.
Rather, these articles will provide a picture of the bird and many
of its features. They will examine the past, present and future of
the turkey, and delve into some of the challenges and rewards the
bird provides. Further, you'll read some strong opinions here
about how we view, manage and understand turkeys.

Above all, this section is designed to pay tribute to the grand
bird that makes the turkey scene possible — the wild turkey.

■ BRIAN LOVETT

CHAPTER 1

Fifty Years and 5 Million Turkeys Later

The author, one of the country's foremost turkey biologists, has a unique personal perspective about the turkey's comeback story.

■ LOVETT E. WILLIAMS JR.

Enormous numbers of wild turkeys co-existed for more than 10,000 years with American Indians in the woodlands of eastern North America.

Then came European settlers.

Man's Killing Fist

Early accounts used terms like "prodigious multitudes" to describe turkey flocks. Then came market hunting, and by the 1700s, turkeys were becoming scarce in the populated Northeastern colonies. They were extirpated in Connecticut by 1813, last seen in New York in 1844 and gone from Massachusetts by 1851. Before the 19th century ended, the symbol of the American Thanksgiving feast remained in only 12 percent of its former range, and was absent from 15 states where it had been abundant. The decline continued into the 20th century.

The year 2000 will mark the 50th anniversary of the lowest ebb in American turkey numbers. The turkey is back, and it's a good time to contemplate and celebrate a remarkable turnaround in American wildlife conservation.

As the 20th century began, year-round hunting, ineffective game laws, one-horse game departments and public indifference to the plight of wildlife were taking their toll. The new nation had the recipe for wildlife disaster on the front burner. Mountainous regions of Pennsylvania and large Southern swamps still held good turkey populations, but why would the fate of these birds differ from the rest? Conservationists predicted turkeys would not be a huntable species anywhere much longer.

When Virginia biologist Henry S. Mosby attempted to gather information about the turkey's population status in 1936, one state game official said his state had no "Eastern wild turkeys," only the "regular old native turkey." The man in charge of the turkey's future didn't know what an Eastern turkey was. Not surprisingly, the turkey — the Eastern and "regular old kind" — continued its decline.

Personal Experience

I was born in 1935 in northern Florida, where many local men hunted and carried guns in the woods year-round. Game was free meat, and numerous citizens pursued it. Unrelenting subsistence hunting, much of it illegal, was taking turkey numbers lower.

An older boy in my neighborhood had a shotgun. Shooting a double-barreled 12-gauge was a two-edged sword for a small 8-year-old, but I endured the recoil and killed a few squirrels. I asked questions about game animals and listened when the old men talked. I heard there were a few turkeys in the area, but the old-timers said I would never see one. In 1943, the turkey was already nearly extirpated in Taylor County, Fla., despite a sparse human population in the cut-over sawmill region.

I've learned since that conservationists faced big problems in the 1930s. First, nobody knew the status of turkeys or other American wildlife. Even if they had known, they wouldn't have known what to do. And there was no money to do anything, anyway.

When things seemed to be at their worst, a conservation movement with important consequences for turkeys was shifting into gear. In 1937, Congress approved the Pittman-Robertson Wildlife Restoration Act, which provided federal money to states to hire biologists and manage wildlife. The money came from an excise tax on guns and ammunition. Also that year, The Wildlife Society was formed with the

objective of professionalizing the wildlife conservation movement.

One of the first products of the Pittman-Robertson program and the new professionalism in wildlife management was the 1943 book *The Wild Turkey in Virginia*, by Henry S. Mosby and C.O. Handley, which reported the first scientific study of turkeys.

The Saga Continues

At the end of World War II, the GI Bill was educating war veterans. College graduates of wildlife conservation programs were taking jobs in state and federal agencies, and wildlife research and management papers were being published in the new *Journal of Wildlife Management*. I was still shooting squirrels, but was large enough to shoot without taking two steps backward. And, as predicted by the old-timers, I had not seen a wild turkey.

In 1948, Florida exchanged its political conservation department for a new commission system designed to move game laws and programs farther from the grasp of the governor and legislature. That year, Florida's wildlife biologists began surveys for the state's first turkey restoration program.

In 1949, I went turkey hunting for the first time. A classmate's grandfather took us to Little River Swamp and positioned me near a creek slough where he said turkeys roosted. I sat like a statue against a cypress tree with my finger on the trigger, and strained my eyes and ears until dark. When the mosquitoes started biting and the owls started hooting, my first turkey hunt was finished. I hadn't seen, heard or shot a turkey, but I had been turkey hunting.

Despite the new wildlife commission system, the politics of wildlife conservation didn't change overnight. Florida's turkey restoration program began with a poor grade of pen-reared turkeys — not because that was the best way, but because the commission chairman owned a game farm. The releases of farm-raised turkeys failed, as biologists had predicted.

The wisdom of following biologists' recommendations was slow to catch on. Throughout the country, unqualified officials used their authority to micromanage wildlife programs. That kept Pennsylvania in the turkey-farm business — despite objections from the state's biologists — for 30 years after the futility of releasing semidomestic turkeys became evident.

A Passion Born

Like an omen, I saw my first wild turkey in May 1952. The lone hen was walking down a logging road near Spring Warrior Creek. At that time, I was old enough to have a driver's license and was back in Taylor County to fish in an old fishing hole. The warmouth perch were biting, but while I fished and swatted yellow flies, I thought mostly about that hen.

Efforts to trap turkeys in the late 1940s and early '50s were earnest but clumsy. Biologists reinvented methods, and tried and improved drop-nets, wire walk-in pens, and pole- and rail-traps. Everybody was working hard, but few were catching many turkeys.

When I graduated from college in 1957, little had been written about turkey biology. To me, the turkey was a bird of great mystique — a denizen of the swamp, known to few and rarely killed except by skilled woodsmen. Some agencies were conducting turkey management, but it seemed nobody was trying to learn about the turkey itself. I believed studying the life and ecology of turkeys would be as much a challenge as hunting turkeys. I went to graduate school in 1958 intent on studying turkeys.

My timing was good. Wildlife management was new, vigorous and on the move in the late '50s. A highlight of my two years at Auburn University was the First National Wild Turkey Symposium, sponsored by The Wildlife Society at the Peabody Hotel in Memphis, Tenn. Turkey managers, biologists and administrators from throughout the country met for two days to share information. By that time, the cannon net had been perfected, and biologists were giving glowing reports about transplanting turkeys. The symposium featured population status reports, food-and-habit studies, and roundtable discussions about everything from game laws to turkey habitat. Almost every Eastern state had a restoration project or was contemplating one.

Success Realized

Fast-forward 10 years to 1969. Florida had just successfully completed its turkey-restoration program with wild-trapped birds, and had turkeys and turkey hunting in every county. One by one, other states completed their restorations, and by 1991, every state except Alaska featured turkey hunting. In 1994, the United States held 4 million turkeys. By the 21st century, the country had about 5 million turkeys. Today, populations are still expanding.

How did this happen? Congress' passage of the Pittman-Robertson Wildlife Restoration Act was critical. The law was written more wisely than most people realize. Funds were specifically restricted for use only in scientific wildlife management projects conducted by qualified personnel — namely biologists and technicians. Without those stipulations, wildlife department administrators, like the official who had only "regular old turkeys" in his state, would still be micromanaging wildlife from the office, and we would still be hearing dire predictions about the turkey's future.

Besides the Pittman-Robertson Act, the first trapping-and-transplant program, in New Mexico during the 1930s, deserves credit. That set the example for future programs. Also, credit the development of the cannon net, which enabled state wildlife personnel to conduct large-scale trapping operations. These biologists performed their jobs well, trapping the thousands of turkeys required for restoration.

The Road Ahead

Wildlife conservation will be more difficult in the 21st century. During the past 300 years, the conservation movement was mostly combating ignorance. During the 21st century, ignorance will be the least of our problems.

We will combat human overpopulation and the calamitous cultural and political changes it will bring. As we enter the 21st century, traditional uses of wildlife are taking a back seat to the needs of the rapidly overpopulating human species. Our values as hunters and outdoorsmen are being exchanged for someone else's.

There is hope, though. Since the National Wild Turkey Federation was founded in 1973, it has grown and matured on the wave of turkey hunting's popularity, and has taken up where conservation's pioneers left off. With its large, enthusiastic and well-organized membership, the group is poised to be a prominent player in preserving the hunting heritage in the 21st century. The NWTF can use all the help it can get —including yours.

The old-timers were wrong in 1943 when they said I wouldn't see a turkey. Their faulty prediction attests to the magnitude of turkey restoration.

Who in 1943 could have predicted that during Thanksgivings in the early 21st century, there would be more wild turkeys on tables than during any previous Thanksgiving?

— Lovett E. Williams Jr., longtime contributing editor for Turkey & Turkey Hunting, *is recognized as one of the country's foremost turkey biologists. He lives in Florida.*

Milestones and Perspectives on Turkey Restoration

1932: The first turkey trap-and-transplant program is initiated in New Mexico.

1935: The author is born. Turkeys are scarce and declining.

1937: The federal Pittman-Robertson Wildlife Restoration Act is enacted. The Wildlife Society is founded.

1943: Mosby and Handley's *The Wild Turkey in Virginia* is published.

1948: Florida forms its first nonpolitical wildlife agency.

1949: The author goes on his first turkey hunt. He doesn't see or hear a turkey.

1950: Florida initiates turkey restoration using pen-reared turkeys — without success.

1951: Florida begins a trap-and-transplant turkey restoration project under the Pittman-Robertson Wildlife Restoration Act. In South Carolina, the cannon net is used successfully on turkeys for first time.

1952: The author sees his first wild turkey.

1955: The author shoots his first wild turkey.

1959: The author receives his MS degree with a thesis on wild turkeys.

1962: The author begins working in wildlife management in Florida. Successful turkey restorations are underway in several states, including Florida.

1969: Florida becomes the first state to complete turkey restoration and has turkeys in every county.

1973: The National Wild Turkey Federation is founded.

1977: The NWTF initiates a program to assist state restoration work.

1991: Turkey hunting is legal in every state except Alaska.

1994: The country's turkey population tops 4 million.

2003: The United States has more turkeys — more than 5 million — than any previous year of the past century.

— Lovett E. Williams Jr.

CHAPTER 2

The Turkey Hunting Chronicles

Within the passage of a generation, turkey hunting has changed dramatically, and those changes are recorded in the sport's magazines.

■ JIM CASADA

Any serious student of the lure and lore of turkey hunting will, upon reflection, suggest there's really nothing new under the sun.

For example, some four score years ago, Archibald Rutledge described calling techniques we now know as the aggressive or fighting purr. Old masters such as Tom Turpin and Henry Edwards Davis left detailed information about set-up and calling strategies many hunters think emerged in the modern era. Further, most basic types of calls have been around for a century or more. Even early versions of the diaphragm can be traced back before the era of turkey restoration.

Yet there is no denying that the way hunters approach the sport has changed dramatically. As historians are fond of saying, "You can't know where you're going if you don't know where you've been." It's easy to follow turkey hunting's evolution by studying the books and magazines that sprang from the fascination hunters and conservationists have with turkeys.

As recently as 30 years ago there were no magazines devoted to the sport, and turkey articles rarely appeared in general outdoor periodicals. In 1950, four books devoted to turkey hunting had been published. Even by 1970, there were only two dozen or so such works.

Today, *Turkey & Turkey Hunting* and the National Wild Turkey Federation's *Turkey Call* cover the turkey scene in detail, and many other publications devote special spring issues to the subject. You can find more than 200 books on turkey hunting, and another 10 or so are published each year.

Big Changes in a Short Time

Within a generation, turkey hunting has changed dramatically, and those changes are chronicled in the sport's magazines. Recently, I leafed through my turkey magazine collection. It was armchair adventure at its finest, and although I've lived and hunted through the period of most dramatic change in the sport, peeking back a couple of decades was a startling reminder and revelation.

For example, the premier issue of *Turkey* (the original title of *T&TH*; see the associated sidebar), which appeared in March 1984, featured only two types of camouflage. Jim Crumley, the pioneer in the field, occupied the back cover with an ad for his breakthrough pattern, Trebark.

Another ad from an outlet specializing in military surplus offered a "genuine woodland camouflage battle dress uniform." That's quite a contrast from today, when there are dozens of camo patterns on the market, including several that have stood the test of time. (Of course, everything is relative. In this case, the test of time is less than two decades.) Many of the hunters pictured in the initial *Turkey* aren't wearing camo, and that was common for several more years.

Today, no turkey hunter would take to the woods without wearing camouflage from head to toe, complete with gloves and a facemask.

Calls were the most commonly advertised products in early magazines. Some names — Lohman, Quaker Boy, Penn's Woods and Tom Gaskins — are still around, but most of the call-makers belong to a lost world. It's also obvious there was a lack of various call types. Boxes dominated. You might find some mention of tube calls or suction yelpers. Similarly, other than an odd mention of an owl hooter or crow call, you couldn't find much information on locator calls.

Really New Additions to the Sport

You couldn't find any early coverage for areas that currently receive lots of attention. Special chokes for turkey guns are a phenomena of the past decade, and that also holds true for gun optics.

Jim Schlender

Brian Lovett

Guns made specifically for turkey hunting, with slings, drastically shortened barrels, super-tight chokes, and camo or matte-black finishes, also arrived on the scene recently. Most old-time hunters used an all-purpose shotgun, such as the reliable Remington Model 870 pump, or opted for a 12-gauge double-barrel with 28- or 30-inch barrels.

Special turkey shotshells evolved at about the same pace as guns. Most old-time hunters shot high-brass loads in their favorite shot size, and you could also find nonsense about No. 2 shot — or even buckshot — being ideal for turkey hunting. Ten-gauges, duplex loads and 3½-inch shells were almost unheard of even 15 years ago.

Accessories many hunters now consider essential received scant mention by the sport's scribes — and I was among their ranks — even as recently as the late 1980s. Some vests were rudimentary at best, and you can find no mention of loungers, special seats, self-supporting vests and the like. Similarly, although most hunters understood that 40 yards was about the maximum distance at which you should shoot a turkey, range-finders were uncommon. Even obvious items like binoculars were commonly overlooked.

The same holds true for decoys, although Harry Williams of Roanoke Rapids, N.C., began making hand-painted decoys around 1970. Also, turkey totes, call carriers and more items weren't mentioned.

Surprisingly, portable blinds were mentioned frequently. Perhaps that reflects the fact that yesterday's hunters typically stayed put more often than today's cutt-and-run crowd.

Books and Videos for Sale

In addition, there was little mention of videotapes in early magazines, although audiocassettes started to appear by the mid-1980s. A 1985 ad for *Spring Gobbler Hunting*, a video from Gulvas Calls, sold for $59.95. The price is interesting, because today's videos — and you'll find scores of them — sell for far less.

That's about the only area in which prices have decreased. Typically, they have increased.

You could buy a copy of Wayne Bailey's *50 Years Hunting Wild Turkeys* or Dwain Bland's *Some Turkey Scratchings* for only $6.95. If you can find a copy of either today, they sell for $150 to $200. Charlie Elliott's little *Field Guide to Wild Turkey Hunting*, an extremely rare volume I've only seen twice in my years of collecting, cost $7.95, with a Penn's Woods diaphragm thrown in. You could buy handcrafted wingbone calls for less than $20 and a camouflage jumpsuit for $19.95.

By today's standards, when hunters eagerly seek literature on advanced calling or special tactics for specific situations,

most stories from two decades ago are pretty straightforward. I think it's fair to say most modern hunters would consider them elementary, but you can find exceptions.

My old buddy Bob Clark, for example, wrote a 1985 article called "Turkey in the Grass" for *Turkey*. It deals with the problems turkey hunters might encounter when running into hidden, booby-trapped patches of marijuana. Generally, though, safety concerns didn't receive the attention they do today, and you'll find frequent mentions of gobble calls as locators without reference to the potential dangers.

Products such as bug suits, camouflage raingear, snakeproof boots, Global Positioning System units, blaze-orange bags and vest flaps, devices to create motion in decoys, waterproof box or friction calls, or locators that sound like peacocks, coyotes or hawks weren't mentioned. Turkey hunting has evolved a great deal and continues to do so.

The Most Dramatic Change

Without question, the most dramatic change — and one that underlies the great comeback of America's big-game bird — is when we hunt turkeys. Until the modern era, turkey hunting was a sport for fall and winter.

Hunting gobblers only in spring is a recent development, but no one can deny the break with tradition worked wonders for the turkey's return. Turkey numbers have increased sufficiently to make fall and winter hunting viable in most states — including some that should offer a return to the sport's roots but have yet to do so.

Success and Continuing Changes

As a diehard traditionalist who loves the past, I'm not always happy with newfangled ways. However, you can't deny the delight hunters should feel when considering how much has changed in such a brief time. That rapid, continuing evolution is directly related to the turkey's great comeback.

That's something everyone who harkens to the sound of a spring gobble or thrills to a scattered flock calling in fall must hail with joy.

— Jim Casada is the editor-at-large for Turkey & Turkey Hunting. *He hails from Rock Hill, S.C.*

Turkey & Turkey Hunting Evolves With the Sport it Covers

The history of *Turkey & Turkey Hunting* and its predecessors is interesting and confusing.

The first *Turkey & Turkey Hunting* appeared in 1991, and only one issue was published. In 1992 and 1993, four issues appeared. Since then, the magazine has published six issues annually. Beginning in 1993, the magazine picked up the numbering system associated with the magazine it superseded, *The Turkey Hunter*. In other words, the six issues that appeared in 1993 comprised Volume 10 of the magazine. To confuse matters more, *The Turkey Hunter* was originally called *Turkey*, with Volumes 1, 2 and 3, along with the first five issues of Volume 4, appearing under that title.

For collectors, here are the details from the first issue of *Turkey* in 1984 to the present. Some early issues are rare, and I don't know of one complete set. My holdings are missing seven or eight issues.

Volumes 1 and 2 (1984-'85 and 1985-'86) were monthly issues.

Volume 3 (1986-'87) comprised 10 issues.

Volume 4 (1987-'88) had eight issues, the final three of which were published as *The Turkey Hunter*.

Volumes 5 through 9 (1988-'92) featured eight issues each year, except for 1989-'90, when only seven appeared. From 1990 onward, the volumes covered the calendar year.

The premier edition of *Turkey & Turkey Hunting* was published in 1991.

Volume 2 (1992-'93) of *Turkey & Turkey Hunting* comprised four issues.

Volume 10 (renumbered for consistency) began in 1993. Krause Publications has published six issues annually since then, with the 2003 magazines comprising Volume 20.

— Jim Casada

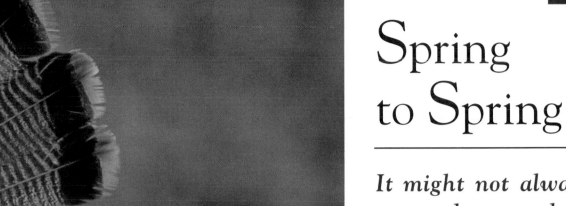

CHAPTER 3

Spring to Spring

It might not always seem true, but turkeys are almost always preparing for spring.

■ *LOVETT E. WILLIAMS JR.*

In a way, turkeys spend their lives anticipating the spring breeding season. During summer, fall and winter, gobblers and hens flock separately, feeding heavily on the seeds of grasses, trees and scrubs to grow new plumage and fatten themselves for spring.

Gobblers store fat mostly in their breast sponges, which lets them go without feed and concentrate on mating during spring. Hens store fat in thick layers under their skin and in deposits among their internal organs in expectation of their confinement to nests. In instinctive anticipation of the laying season, hens seek food rich in minerals — especially calcium — for egg-shell formation. Studies indicate hens eat more snails in late winter and spring than during the rest of the year, and more than the gobblers ever eat.

By winter's end, the abundant, easily found foods of fall and early winter are almost exhausted. Resourceful turkeys scratch a few acorns and find some other favorite foods, but they must settle for more variety and diminishing quantities, and they eat items they pass up in fall.

Spring's warm weather brings new food. Where sunshine reaches the ground, turkeys find succulent buds, flowers, insects and fresh seed pods. As these foods become more abundant, turkeys in forested landscapes shift their ranges from increasingly shaded deep-woods areas to sunny fields and open places. They might move long distances from winter to spring ranges.

Gobblers Break Up, Call Hens

Along with shifts in home ranges, turkeys exhibit social changes in spring.

Initial early-spring gobbling is accompanied by fighting, as gobblers adjust their social order for the mating season. Disagreements increase, fighting intensifies, and winter gobbler flocks break into smaller units.

Adult gobblers travel alone or in alliances of twos and threes during the breeding season. They continue to use much of their former range but disperse somewhat at this time.

When a spring tom is in the mood, he gobbles to announce his location and interest in mating. Hens can hear gobbling from the roost from longer distances than gobbling from the ground. It's not surprising perfect spring days begin with lots of gobbling from the roost.

Hunters enjoy spring seasons because gobbling lets them know where turkeys are. You might not see or hear an old gobbler all winter, but when gobbling begins, longbeards seem to be everywhere.

Also, gobblers suddenly gain interest in a hen's voice. You can call your head off in fall and not hear a cluck from an adult tom. In spring, however, even the most hardened old longbeard will raise his head at a hen's calling. He might not always come in strutting, but that's not the way the mating process works. Then again, he might come in strutting.

Brian Lovett

Two Peaks or One?

The seasonal gobbling pattern has long been an enigma to hunters and biologists. Scientists have two prevalent peak theories.

One viewpoint holds that early-season gobbling begins before hens have an interest in mating, and peaks as gobblers call more in hopes of attracting hens, which don't come. When hens finally come to gobblers, it stimulates toms to strut more and gobble less, resulting in a gobbling lull. That's when most copulation is believed to occur.

When hens begin to desert spring mating flocks and strike out alone to nest, toms gobble more in a vain effort to call hens back. Ostensibly, the increased gobbling produces a second, and somewhat greater, gobbling peak. A South Carolina study supports this two-peak theory, and field observations from biologists in Pennsylvania, Virginia and West Virginia have also reported two peaks. An Ohio study suggested there might be three peaks.

A less widely held view maintains there's only one gobbling peak. Biologists in Alabama concluded that many years ago, and a recent Mississippi field study supports the one-peak theory.

A Sensible Theory

I believe single peaks occur at some times and places, but other areas sometimes experience additional peaks. What an area experiences depends on local circumstances, including the date, seasonal temperatures, the number of gobblers and the social activities of turkeys. These can occur in combinations that increase or diminish gobbling. Also, hunting can modify would-be natural peaks, because it can cause the sudden deaths of toms that gobble most or come eagerly to imitated hen calling.

The two-peak theory holds logic. Toms gobble less when they're strutting with hens. If gobbler numbers are low, it seems likely most longbeards would be occupied with hens during the mating peak, which would limit gobbling. That might be true in heavily hunted areas with many more hens than gobblers.

However, if a population includes many adult gobblers, the lull caused by strutting might give way to increased gobbling as the season progresses, because many toms wouldn't have hens.

What statisticians call sample size also affects perceived peaks. If you hunt where gobbling is good several consecutive days, you would consider that a peak. However, someone else — even in the same county — might have different luck. That also applies to researchers. Biologists need more study on gobbling and the factors that affect it before they can be certain about a theory. The single- and double-peak theories might each be true.

Breeding Flocks Form

As spring days become longer, winter hen flocks dissolve. Gobbling begins to pay off, as hens begin to associate with toms. Where turkeys are plentiful, large, loosely organized mating flocks form. Hens in mating flocks have no social relationship with each other, and their comings and goings changes mating flock numbers almost daily. Gobblers have a strict pecking order, and only one in a group will mate. Other gobblers act as bodyguards and help with gobbling and strutting. Some jakes usually live on the fringes of mating flocks, but are unwelcome and have no role in mating.

Turkey hens are promiscuous, and it's misleading to think of a spring mating flock as a harem. There's no evidence a hen is faithful to one gobbler or tied to a specific mating flock. When a hen in a mixed-sex group is ready to mate, she squats for the dominant gobbler, and they copulate.

Soon after copulating, hens look for nesting cover and sometimes travel considerable distances. Some gobblers usually move with them. Nesting hens often travel to places they would shun during other seasons. Hens don't have time to eat after they begin incubating eggs and must live off stored fat. Gobblers have stored enough fat in their breast sponges, so they look for and follow hens.

Food availability doesn't affect the location of hens during nesting, and no amount of feeding or food plots keep hens from moving to suitable nesting habitat.

The Courting Season Ends

As hens begin to nest, they stop associating with gobblers, and mixed-sex mating flocks diminish and gradually disap-pear. Small gobbler mating alliances combine into larger flocks, similar to groups before the spring breakup. This happens in June in the South and July farther north. Gobbler flocks are larger than they are in winter if toms permit jakes to join. However, most flocks are smaller because some gobblers are dead. Most jakes remain in jake-only groups to form their own adult gobbler flocks the next season.

While gobbler flocks reform, hens incubate eggs. Hens that didn't nest group together and are joined by hens that nested unsuccessfully. These broodless hens won't associate with family flocks.

Turkeys change plumage every summer, but molting isn't physiologically compatible with turkeys' mating hormone regime and doesn't begin until the breeding season is finished. Because jakes don't usually mate, they molt first. Even during spring hunting season, jakes begin their annual molt by shedding some wingfeathers. When molting finishes in fall, last spring's jakes will be adult gobblers in every respect.

Older gobblers start molting when they end their quest for hens. Their new plumage looks the same as the previous year's, but their beards and spurs grow longer. Hens don't molt until they end nesting attempts for the year. When they do, they molt faster than gobblers.

Summer Returns

Summer produces good foraging conditions in prairies, meadows, wood edges, open areas and wooded roads, where birds can find insects, berries, leaves and succulent plant buds.

Turkey populations peak in early summer. Numbers decline steadily as winter approaches. By winter's end, the population reaches its annual low point. Then, flocks again dissolve, home ranges shift, toms gobble, adults mate, jakes watch, and hens nest and renew population numbers.

— *Lovett E. Williams Jr., longtime contributing editor for* Turkey & Turkey Hunting, *is recognized as one of the country's foremost turkey biologists. He lives in Florida.*

CHAPTER 4

Diseases:
Ways Wild
Turkeys Die

Turkeys die many ways, but mostly from predation, trauma — including hunting mortality — and diseases. We know a lot about predation and trauma, but turkey diseases remain somewhat enigmatic.

■ GEORGE A. HURST

Jan. 14, 1984, was a cold, rainy day, so John Goodman decided to ride around his cattle ranch near Kewanee, Miss. He hadn't traveled far when he saw a large gobbler standing in a pasture. The tom's wings were dropped, and its head and neck were bent over. It didn't respond to screams or horn blasts. Goodman walked within 10 feet of the gobbler, but it didn't budge.

Then, Goodman remembered an article he had read. Someone nicknamed "Turkey Man" — OK, it's me — at Mississippi State University wanted people to pick up sick, dying or dead turkeys and call him.

Goodman called a conservation officer, and the men easily caught the gobbler. The bird had a 10-inch beard and 1-inch spurs but weighed just 13 pounds. It was later determined the turkey had listeriosis, which is caused by the bacterium *Listeria monocytogenes*. No wild turkey in the United States had ever died from listeriosis, and no other cases of the disease have been documented since 1984.

Ways Turkeys Die

In the early 1980s, the Mississippi Department of Wildlife, Fisheries and Parks began a statewide program with MSU's College of Veterinary Medicine to monitor wildlife diseases using animals killed by hunters and vehicles. Through television and magazines, coordinators asked farmers, landowners, foresters and hunters to capture sick or recently killed turkeys and contact me, other biologists or a wildlife conservation officer. The DWFP then transported sick or dead turkeys to the College of Veterinary Medicine, where biologists performed necropsies, which are detailed examinations of an animal's external and internal parts.

As part of the necropsies, examiners sent tissue samples from the turkeys' major organs to specialists who obtained microscopic samples, such as bacteria or viruses. Also, examiners took X-rays to determine if trauma such as a collision or gunshot killed a bird. An avian pathologist prepared a final report and, if possible, diagnosed the cause of illness or death.

Why the interest? A veterinarian once said, "George, you have to understand that turkeys like to die. They will find a way to die."

I agreed. Turkeys die many ways, but mostly from predation, trauma — including hunting mortality — and diseases. We know a lot about predation and trauma, but turkey diseases remain somewhat enigmatic.

Avian Pox

Several years ago, a hunter found a sick hen standing on a roadside. The bird was blind, and her head was covered with ugly sores and scabs. The hunter caught the hen, put her in a bag and called me. Examinations revealed the hen was suffering from avian pox, a common wild turkey disease.

Avian pox is an infectious disease caused by the virus *Avipoxvirus*. It's also known as fowl pox and sore-head. Turkeys with avian pox usually have sores, lesions and scabs on their naked skin areas, such as the head, neck, legs and feet. Also, birds suffer from weakness, emaciation, blindness and respiratory distress.

Avian pox has two forms: dry and wet. If the virus only invades a turkey's outer skin, it's classified as dry, and its harmfulness varies. Turkeys infected with dry avian pox might die, but many survive and recover. If the disease strikes both of a bird's eyes and the turkey becomes blind, predators or scavengers will kill it. However, project workers have captured turkeys that have recovered from dry avian pox.

If avian pox involves a bird's mouth, throat or trachea, it's called wet pox. Turkeys with wet pox cannot eat, and soon become emaciated and weak. They starve or are killed by predators.

Avipoxvirus is primarily transmitted by mosquitoes. A mosquito that feeds on the blood of an infected bird can transfer the virus to another turkey. The number of pox infections might be related to rainfall and mosquito hatches. I've seen avian pox cases from late winter through early fall.

Avian pox can also be transferred if the virus is rubbed into abraded skin from sores of an infected bird.

Avian pox cannot be controlled in wild birds. It's always present in turkey populations but never becomes an epidemic. Typically, you find infected birds scattered throughout turkey range.

Blackhead Disease

In 1989, a county agent in southwestern Mississippi told me farmers were seeing lots of sick turkeys in their fields. That was bad news. Turkey densities in the area had increased through the 1980s, and hunters commonly reported hearing or seeing numerous birds. However, the reports indicated blackhead disease —the scourge of wild turkeys — was becoming an epidemic in the region.

Blackhead disease is no stranger to Mississippi, but it was usually found in turkeys along the Mississippi River. In 1980, I wrote a paper for the *Journal of Wildlife Diseases* about four turkeys that died of blackhead disease. Now, I was hearing about many turkeys dying.

Turkeys that die from blackhead disease don't have a black head. Rather, they become emaciated, and might have chalky, yellowish material around their cloaca, which is a bird's anal vent.

Blackhead disease, or histomoniasis, is caused by the protozoan parasite *Histomonas meleagris*. It is carried by the nematode cecal worm *Heterakis gallinarum*. This roundworm lives in the ceca, or two blind pouches off the large intestine, of wild turkeys. The histomonad parasites invade a turkey's ceca and infect female nematodes. Histomonads might be incorporated into nematode eggs, which are passed on when an infected turkey defecates. If the egg-bearing scat is near

vegetation or a feed pile, the disease can easily be passed to other turkeys. If turkeys eat the heterakid eggs, the eggs hatch, and the histomonads are released in the ceca. Turkeys can also ingest cecal worms and histomonad parasites by eating earthworms.

The histomonads invade the bird's ceca, producing inflammation, ulceration, hemorrhage and necrosis, or tissue death. This causes a turkey to become ill. However, it gets worse. Histomonads enter the turkey's blood system and are carried to the liver. There, they quickly multiply, causing severe inflammation, necrosis and death.

Turkeys are highly susceptible to blackhead disease, and usually suffer a high death rate from it.

During blackhead epidemics, observers typically see many sick turkeys standing around, or acting "droopy." In 1990, hunters reported seeing five droopy turkeys along a field edge in Amite County, Miss.

The Spread of Blackhead

Some turkeys infected with blackhead survive and support cecal worms that produce histomonad-bearing eggs. This maintains blackhead disease in turkey populations.

Turkey populations slowly recover after blackhead epidemics. As bird numbers increase, the chance of the disease occurring and spreading increases. The higher the concentration of turkeys, the greater the probability of blackhead becoming a limiting factor.

Can managers control blackhead? They can try by recommending either-sex fall hunting in areas with high turkey densities. Also, they might recommend that people don't release pen-raised turkeys, and keep other fowl — such as chickens, pheasants or pen-raised quail — out of the wild. These birds can transmit blackhead to turkeys.

Aspergillosis

Before 1995, researchers had only documented one case of aspergillosis in a wild turkey. However, the MSU team documented two cases that year.

A deer hunter found a sick hen standing along a woodland road in Leake County, Miss. The hunter put the hen in a dog box and called me. An officer rushed the hen to the college, where the necropsy team diagnosed the bird's cause of death as multifocal pyogranulomatous — inflammation of the lungs and air sac associated with aspergillosis.

Aspergillosis is a fungal disease caused by *Aspergillus fumigatus*. The disease typically begins with an infection in the respiratory tract, but it might also infect other organs.

Aspergillus fumigatus is distributed throughout turkey range. However, wildlife managers have become increasingly concerned about the fungus because it's often present on moldy corn. It grows best on decomposing organic matter, such as corn piles in warm, moist environments. Turkeys become infected with aspergillosis by breathing in fungal spores while feeding on moldy corn.

Because of this, moldy corn, peanuts or grains should never be used as turkey feed. However, corn is the food of choice for baiters and feeders. Baiting, which is illegal in Mississippi, is prevalent during deer season and, to a lesser degree, turkey season.

An aspergillosis-infected turkey becomes emaciated and has difficulty breathing, and gapes or gasps for breath. These birds die from acute respiratory distress and failure. The hens we diagnosed in 1995 had chronic infections. However, turkeys can also develop acute cases, which suddenly kill birds that are otherwise in good shape.

Aflatoxicosis

The corn-disease problem might worsen. Two other fungi, *Aspergillus flauus* and *Aspergillus parasiticus*, might cause aflatoxicosis. Corn and other grains infected by these fungi contain anatoxins. Wildlife ingest the toxins by eating infected grain.

Biologists haven't attributed any turkey deaths to aflatoxicosis, but research at the University of Georgia's Southeastern Cooperative Wildlife Disease Study recently determined 4-month-old pen-raised turkeys fed various levels — 100, 200 and 400 parts per billion — of aflatoxin ate less and gained less weight, and experienced immune system maladies and decreased liver weights and functions.

Birds are more sensitive to aflatoxins than mammals, and wild birds are probably more sensitive than pen-raised birds. Don't feed or bait turkeys with corn or other grains that might have high 100 ppb or higher aflatoxin concentrations. The U.S. Food and Drug Administration monitors aflatoxin levels in corn intended for consumption by humans or domestic animals. The agency prohibits the use of corn with aflatoxin levels that exceed federal standards. However, corn that cannot be fed to pigs can be purchased and fed to turkeys. Is this another way for turkeys to die?

Lympho-Proliferative Disease

In Fall 1988, Skip Jack of MSU's College of Veterinary Medicine called me.

"Turkey Man, you have another first, another national record," he said.

A turkey recently brought to the college had died of a lymphoid neoplastic process, or lymphoproliferative disease, or lympho. Lympho had been reported in some hybrid commercial turkeys, but had never been identified in wild turkeys.

The disease is caused by a retrovirus and is spread through contact. Its most obvious symptom is an enlarged liver, which is often pale or marbled. Turkeys afflicted with lympho die suddenly.

During the next two years, biologists identified 10 cases of lympho in Mississippi turkeys. The National Vet Services Lab confirmed the diagnoses. At about the same time, an Alabama veterinarian told me he had determined lympho had killed several turkeys in his state.

The wild turkey had found another way to die.

Other Diseases

Mycoplasmosis, a disease caused by the bacteria *Mycoplasma gallisepticum*, hasn't been found in wild turkeys in Mississippi. However, this deadly disease has been identified in barnyard chickens in the region.

Salmonella can be found everywhere, but doesn't cause problems for turkeys. A secondary salmonellosis contributed to the death of one wild turkey.

Coccidiosis killed 18 captive, pen-raised turkeys at MSU, but it hasn't been diagnosed in wild turkeys.

I've also seen several cases of a bacterial infection called bumblefoot, in which a bird's feet appear to be decaying.

Conclusion

How can you help? Reading this article is a start.

Also, you can help by not baiting, feeding and concentrating turkeys near feeders or small food plots. In addition, capture sick turkeys, and take them to a veterinarian. Further, realize that although high turkey populations are great for hunting, they invite disease.

Lastly, don't panic and think the aforementioned diseases will significantly harm turkey numbers. Turkeys find many ways to die, as a recent phone call reminded me.

"Turkey Man?" the voice on the phone said. "I heard you want dead turkeys. Well, I got three gobblers this spring, and I'm damn sure they died of lead poisoning, if you know what I mean."

This is still the No. 1 way gobblers die.

— Wildlife biologist George Hurst studied turkeys for years at Mississippi State University. Although retired, he remains active in wildlife research.

CHAPTER 5

Wariness and Defensive Behavior

Not every turkey passes the test, but every turkey generation must. Those that don't become fossils.

■ *Lovett E. Williams Jr.*

The turkey is a prey species, sought from the egg to adulthood by many predators. About one-half of turkey nests are destroyed before hatching, and many poults succumb to predators before they're two weeks old. Survivors are hunted day and night by skilled, hungry meat-eaters.

The turkey's high reproductive rate partly offsets such losses, but rapid reproduction isn't enough. To survive as a species, turkeys must depend on their wariness, a trait for which it is widely respected. Not every turkey passes the test, but every turkey generation must. Those that don't become fossils.

Sharp Eyes

I learned about the turkey's defensive behavior as a young hunter, and later gained deeper insights through field studies as a biologist. One lesson occurred while I was radio-tracking a turkey brood soon after it hatched. The hen had been wearing a small transmitter since before nesting, and researchers were monitoring the poults.

A heavy thunderstorm hit the night after the brood left the nest, and I needed to count the surviving poults. At midmorning, I moved through the swamp toward the radio signal's source. The brood was on the move. When the signal indicated the brood was near, I stopped to adjust the instrument. The hen had also stopped moving, and I knew I was close. I took a bearing on the signal and scanned the ground in the direction indicated. There she was, in short grass and weeds, about 30 feet away, hunkered over her poults and staring me straight in the eye.

Although I hadn't moved for almost two minutes, the hen had remained still until I spotted her. When I did, pandemonium broke. She screamed and ran circles around me. The poults scattered and hid in the grass. I searched and counted. All the poults had survived the storm, and each was dry.

I moved into cover to watch the hen assemble the brood and to take notes. Apparently, the hen had seen me before I saw her. That caused her to stop moving and squat over the poults. As I approached, she could tell I hadn't spotted her yet and was hoping I wouldn't. She must have been watching my eyes.

My thoughts were interrupted by a three-note lost-whistle from one of the poults. Another poult whistled, and soon they were all calling. At the sound of the hen's brood-assembly yelp, the whistling stopped. One more whistle echoed, and the hen made one more call. I watched the radio signal weaken as the assembled brood moved deeper into the swamp.

In the subsequent weeks, I observed other young broods. The hens would stop moving and wait for my approach, crouching over their poults. If I simply passed by, a hen would hold her position. But when our eyes met, she would squeal and squawk. I was being perceived as a predator because I was acting like one.

Suspect Everyone

Identifying a predator by its behavior is the *modus operandi* for turkeys. However, a turkey cannot instinctively identify every predator. For a turkey to acquire predator recognition through learning, each must survive hazardous attacks by each predator type. Fortunately for turkeys, a predator in any disguise is recognizable by its predatory nature and is viewed as a threat.

But turkeys seem to be especially cautious of certain predator forms. A snake at close range will put a turkey into near hysteria. Turkeys — even young poults — immediately recognize a hawk flying as a hazard. These are universal predator forms many prey species fear.

Turkeys also acquire wary behavior through experience and close association with older turkeys. I learned this while watching summer broods feeding after a heavy rain. Several broods were eating insects on the shallow water's surface in a grassy glade. One brood, about three months old, had no hen with it. I was able to approach within 50 feet of that brood several times to test its tolerance. It showed concern only when I approached to within 100 yards. The broods with hens reacted at greater distances, probably because the hens had experience with humans.

Turkeys can become less wary of humans when they're not molested, but it takes time to establish such trust. I once watched a ranch manager feeding wild turkeys. When he rattled shelled corn in a coffee can, 40 or more turkeys, adult gobblers included, came within 10 feet of him. When I came out of hiding, the turkeys quickly retreated. The turkeys only trusted the rancher, not humans in general.

Learning to Trust

Wild turkeys can be tamed only by parental-imprinting on humans. Hatchlings instinctively associate their identity with the first large moving object they see at hatching. Under natural circumstances, that would be their mother. However, if turkey eggs are hatched in an artificial incubator, the first large moving thing they see will most likely be a human. If the human stays close by for the next three days, the poults will imprint mentally on the human, and will consider the human their mother.

The mental image created through imprinting is permanent, and imprinted turkeys will never fear any human. That's probably how wild turkeys were domesticated by Indians in Mexico years ago.

What about the sounds humans make? Wild turkeys are temporarily alarmed by any sounds, but will tolerate harmless

without flying, most moved well out of sight before slowing to a walk. They usually proceeded about 300 yards before resuming normal activities. But they remained cautious.

I have also observed the behavior of hotly pursued turkeys. After being flushed from trees by hunters three or four times in rapid succession, radio-tracked turkeys would sometimes fly to the ground and hide in dense thickets — places turkeys would normally shun. A turkey hiding in a thicket could be approached within 30 feet, and it never moved. When pressed closer, it would usually run away rather than fly.

In another study, an adult gobbler that had been shot at on the roost and flushed repeatedly by hunters was found roosting on the ground. To be certain he was not wounded, we approached him and saw him run away without indicating injury. Two nights later, he was roosting in trees again in the same home range.

Conclusion

Such behavior is logical. Alertness and caution are mandatory, and behavioral adjustments are sometimes necessary to avoid harm.

However, nothing in the turkey's evolutionary history has required it to move more than a few yards to avoid an enemy. Predators have never been known to saturate an area, and the impulse to desert a predator-infested place, such as public hunting land, isn't in the turkey's genetic code.

Even if a turkey wanted to leave, it wouldn't know where the danger ends and the safety zone begins. It would never travel in random directions to evade a perceived risk. That would only present new dangers.

Nature is smarter than that.

— Lovett E. Williams Jr., longtime contributing editor for Turkey & Turkey Hunting, *is recognized as one of the country's foremost turkey biologists. He lives in Florida.*

ones such as trains, airplanes, highway noise and distant explosions. I have seen turkeys feeding within 200 yards of the testing grounds for rocket engines.

The turkey's fear of human disturbance has often been overstated. Radio telemetry studies have revealed turkeys are reluctant to abandon their home ranges to elude humans, even when they face hunting pressure. In a Florida study, after most turkeys had been killed during fall turkey hunting on public land, surviving turkeys continued to use their home ranges despite the presence of hunters.

In another study, spring gobblers were shot at and deliberately missed while on their morning roosts to test their reactions. The gobblers flew at the sound of the gun, but most gobbled later in the morning. None deserted the area.

Run for Cover, Not Escape

I have monitored turkey escape behavior when radio-tracking birds. Those startled by hunters flew about 200 to 300 yards, landed in trees and sat for about one hour. After flying down, they resumed normal activities. When turkeys ran

CHAPTER 6

The Royal Slam

North America's five subspecies of wild turkeys are similar yet different. Get to know the birds of the royal slam.

■ *Lovett E. Williams Jr.*

When you discuss a grand slam or a royal slam, be ready to explain the differences between turkey subspecies.

North America holds five wild turkey subspecies: Eastern, Merriam's, Gould's, Osceola and Rio Grande. Easterns, Merriam's, Osceolas and Rio Grandes are common in regions of the United States.

Gould's are common in Mexico, but only a few live in the United States. They can only be hunted in Mexico.

Another wild turkey subspecies, the small ocellated turkey, lives in southern Mexico and Central America.

You accomplish a grand slam when you kill each of the four United States subspecies. Add a Gould's, and you achieve a royal slam. You must add an ocellated turkey for a world slam.

Geographical Distinctions

Like varieties of cattle, wild turkey subspecies sometimes interbreed if they inhabit the same region. However, turkey subspecies usually breed "true" because they are usually geographically separated. Separation acts as an isolating factor, and makes subspecies a geographic phenomenon as much as a genetic phenomenon.

The current distribution of subspecies has been affected by transfers of wild stock. In some areas, subspecies have been introduced where a different subspecies previously existed.

If you hunt outside a subspecies' natural range, you won't have a legitimate grand slam experience. For example, if you take a Rio Grande in California, many people believe it shouldn't count toward a grand slam.

When planning royal slam hunting trips, use reliable range maps, and avoid regions where different subspecies have replaced the originals.

Physical features also distinguish each subspecies.

Eastern

The Eastern turkey — *Meleagris gallopavo silvestris* — has brown-tipped rump feathers and tail margins. The only subspecies with similar markings is the Osceola, or Florida, turkey. Rio Grande, Merriam's, and Gould's turkeys have white or off-white tail margins.

Hunters can distinguish between Easterns and Osceolas by the relative amount of black-and-white barring on the flight feathers of their wings. An Eastern's white wing bars are equal in width to its black wing bars. An Osceola's white wing bars are more narrow than its black bars.

Also, an Osceola's white wing bars are broken, and few extend across the wing.

Osceola

The Osceola — *Meleagris gallopavo osceola* — is smaller than other subspecies.

Osceolas are distinguished from Easterns by the dark barring of their wingfeathers. They can be distinguished from other subspecies by their brown tail margins.

Also, an Osceola's plumage is somewhat darker than other subspecies.

Rio Grande

The Rio Grande — *Meleagris gallopavo intermedia* — lives in the southwestern United States and northeastern Mexico. It is intermediate in appearance between Easterns, Merriam's and Gould's.

The best way to distinguish a Rio Grande from other subspecies is the color of its tail margin and rump feathers. A Rio Grande's tail margins and rump feathers are much lighter than those of Osceolas and Easterns, and are darker than the margins and rumps of Merriam's or Gould's.

Although Rio Grandes exhibit color variability, I haven't seen a Rio Grande that couldn't be distinguished from an Eastern by its lighter rump and tail margin.

Merriam's

The Merriam's is native to the ponderosa pine foothills of the southern Rocky Mountains. It has been successfully stocked in the northern Rockies, the Pacific states, east of the Rockies in Nebraska and in the Northwest.

Recent evidence suggests that Merriam's descended from birds raised in captivity by early American Indians. Fossil records indicate there were no wild turkeys in the southern Rockies before American Indians settled there thousands of years ago. American Indians probably bought or traded tame turkeys from Mexican Indians. Apparently, some of the stock escaped and went wild.

Brian Lovett: Merriam's subspecies

American Indian culture in the southern Rockies — and its domestic turkeys — died before Europeans arrived. The only survivors are Merriam's.

Merriam's have white margins on their rump feathers and tails. That distinguishes them from Easterns and Osceolas, which have brown tail margins, and from Rio Grandes, which have light tan margins.

Merriam's and Gould's have similar plumage. However, it's usually not difficult to distinguish them. Merriam's don't exist in Mexico. Gould's are common in Mexico, but only a few live in the United States, near the Mexican border. They cannot be hunted in the United States.

Physical differences also distinguish Merriam's and Gould's. The tail margins of most Merriam's are not as white as the margins of Gould's. Also, the white tail rim of a Merriam's isn't as wide as a Gould's. If a bird's outer tail margin has a yellow tint, it's a Merriam's.

Also, a Merriam's gobbler's lower legs are shorter than 6 inches, and their toes have little black pigment. Even the smallest Gould's, including spring jakes, have legs longer than 6 inches, and their toes are almost black.

Many adult Merriam's have brownish legs. I have dissected legs of Merriam's gobblers from Colorado, and found that the underlying pigment is as red as that of other subspecies. Apparently, the red is sometimes masked by dark pigmentation in the leg scales.

Gould's

The Gould's is native to the mountains and oak-pine foothills of northwestern Mexico. The species' original museum specimens were taken by a zoologist named Gould, and his name became the subspecies' vernacular. I believe "Mexican wild turkey" would be more appropriate. Some old books refer to Gould's as "Sierra Madre" turkeys.

As previously discussed, the tips of a Gould's rump feathers and tail feathers are pure white. Gould's have long legs and, usually, black toes.

Gould's are the largest subspecies in terms of skeleton size and average weight. Their lower legs and feet are immense. Some say a Gould's plumage has a blue-green tint, but the Gould's I have seen alive and freshly killed were no greener than other subspecies.

— *The author, a contributing editor for* Turkey & Turkey Hunting, *has taken all five North American wild turkey subspecies.*

CHAPTER 7

Whither the Osceola?

Like their American Indian namesake 100 years ago, Florida turkeys face a hazy future.

■ *LOVETT E. WILLIAMS JR.*

I remember when you couldn't find turkeys in Florida far from a swamp. Large swamps gave turkeys sanctuary from year-round subsistence hunting, which often featured illegal baiting and always involved roost-shooting. Thankfully, Florida has enough swamps.

The Florida turkey's historic dependence on swamps is something it has in common with its namesake, Osceola, the Seminole. And like their namesake more than 100 years ago, Florida turkeys face a clouded future.

Florida's Former Scene

Turkeys were absent from four Florida counties and some other large areas of the state when the Florida Game and Fresh Water Fish Commission started turkey restoration work in 1950. The program first used pen-reared turkeys at the insistence of the appointed game commissioner, who owned a game farm. When the pen-reared stock failed — as predicted by biologists — the agency switched to trapped wild turkeys. By the 1970s, every Florida county and all large tracts of wild land held turkeys and featured turkey hunting, except for the treeless Everglades, which never had turkey habitat.

Brian Lovett

Turkeys and much of Florida's other wildlife were traditionally incidental products of timber land, cattle range and tracts of idle woodlands. Nowadays, however, much of Florida's best turkey habitat has been clear-cut for pine monoculture, or converted to airports, residential subdivisions, trailer parks, and for the extensive infrastructure required to support the state's more than 13 million permanent residents, and millions of tourists and winter residents.

As Florida becomes increasingly urbanized, wildlife management and hunting have been trivialized. Wildlife management is of little importance in state affairs, and ranks below other environmental problems that more directly affect the health and welfare of the state's huge, growing population of non-hunting residents.

They Don't Make More Habitat

Florida's large public land acquisition programs, although laudable, provide little help to turkeys because they emphasize preserving wetlands. Most of the protection Florida's government gives to wetlands is apparently intended to accommodate further development by providing unlimited fresh water for additional residents and tourists.

Even when the state buys uplands, it uses only minimal stewardship on them, because the responsible agencies aren't given management money. Turkeys and other wildlife would benefit from greater emphasis on stewardship of state-controlled tracts. However, only 1 percent of Florida voters buy hunting licenses, and it shows.

Florida holds a winter turkey population of about 100,000 making Osceolas the least abundant of North America's five subspecies. The relatively low population is partly the result of the Osceolas' limited range. The state actually holds many excellent turkey populations. In fact, Florida's turkey population has held its own recently — despite habitat loss — almost entirely because of three factors:

✔ Conservation hunting practices on large wooded tracts owned by hunters or leased by hunting clubs.

✔ A drastic decline in subsistence hunting.

✔ A recent regulation protecting hens during fall hunting.

However, there's no way to increase turkey habitat in Florida, nor hope of abating the unrelenting devastation of remaining habitat. Florida's land is worth too much for development and too little for wildlife, cattle, hardwood timber or almost anything else. Idle land is a tax liability in Florida.

Unfortunately, biologists have no dependable management options to offset habitat loss.

Brian Lovett

Brian Lovett

Out of Options?

Most private Florida habitat is near its carrying capacity for turkeys. The few land-management practices ostensibly used to increase turkey numbers have never been tested and probably don't accomplish their intended purpose. Plantings of seedling hardwood trees, the introduction of exotic food plants, or planting annual cultivated food plots won't increase turkey populations. Controlled burning and mowing, which benefit habitat maintenance, can increase turkey numbers only where habitat has been seriously neglected and turkey numbers are low.

It's pointless to try new management ideas without research to determine their cost-effectiveness. However, Florida hasn't had a turkey research program for 15 years.

Harvest management has always been the most powerful tool of game management, but the subject has received scant research attention. An early-1970s Florida study on a public area indicated turkey crippling losses equaled about 25 percent of the harvest on the property. That loss is greater than any management procedure can offset. However, no one has conducted a study to determine how to reduce that appalling waste level.

What Can Be Done?

Even without research, Florida could enact common-sense measures to help turkeys.

For example, the absence of weapons regulations could be corrected with a pen stroke by Florida's autonomous wildlife agency. Currently in Florida, it's legal to shoot at turkeys — I stress at — with almost any weapon. It's legal to use 22-caliber rimfire rifles, even with short cartridges, even though 22s have no shocking power, and cannot disable a turkey except with a shot in the brain or spinal column. High-powered deer rifles are also legal for turkeys, even though they blow apart turkey carcasses. For shotguns, BBs, buckshot, rifled slugs and No. 9 or smaller shot are legal.

So what about the future? Hunters with access to private land will continue to enjoy excellent turkey hunting in Florida. However, inexpensive public hunting will decrease even more.

The Game and Fresh Water Fish Commission is trying desperately to find ways to hold on to land it leases for public hunting, but there's little hope of doing that for long. Several more land-owning corporations recently announced plans to withdraw large acreages from Florida's public hunting area system.

Florida's conservation agencies could do better jobs, but they're not entirely to blame for the dismal future facing turkey hunting in the state. The basic problem is that Florida is overpopulated with people, who come to play, live and make as much money as they can from all the people.

Conclusion

The Seminole American Indian named Osceola suffered great injustices, and died young at the hands of white settlers who encroached on Florida during the mid-1800s.

The name Osceola might be more appropriate for Florida's turkeys than anybody could have guessed more than 100 years ago.

— Lovett E. Williams Jr., a longtime contributing editor for Turkey & Turkey Hunting, *is recognized as one of the country's top turkey biologists. He hails from Florida.*

CHAPTER 8

To Kill a Jake: Should Young Toms be Passed Up?

Typically, killing jakes doesn't harm turkey populations, and many hunters believe killing jakes is a great way to introduce novice hunters to the sport. For some, however, only longbeards generate enough excitement.

■ *TERRY MADEWELL*

Sunrise had passed without a gobble. The rush prompted by the few long-distance gobbles we'd heard had subsided after an arduous 15-minute walk toward the source. My partner, a first-time turkey hunter, was impatient. I stopped every 200 yards to call, but received no answers. I was content with the morning's progress, but my companion was primed for action.

Brian Lovett

I was halfway through a series of yelps when I saw my friend's expression change. I hadn't heard the gobble, but based on his description, the bird was just beyond the next ridge, about 80 yards away.

We quickly set up against a big white oak, and I scratched a soft yelp on my friction call. The gobbler's response echoed through the fresh leaves. The tom was cranking up, and my partner was excited.

Judging from the gobbles, I figured the bird was moving slowly toward us. I believed it would at least get close enough for a shot. I told my friend to shoot at the bird's neck and head when the tom walked within 35 yards.

Minutes later, the bird crossed the ridge in full strut, and my rush faltered. It was a jake.

The jake walked toward us, and then stopped and gobbled in gun range. My heart sank. It was the same gobble we'd been hearing.

I looked at my friend, unsure about what to tell him. Although he was in good position, his left knee was jerking like he was sitting on an ice pack. His breathing was labored, his hands were trembling, and his eyes were transfixed on the target. Because I had instructed him to be sure not to shoot a hen, I knew he was awaiting my instructions. The decision was simple.

"It's the gobbler — take him now!" I said. I had barely spoken when the roar of my buddy's shotgun echoed through the woods. He raced to the turkey, picked up the bird and admired his trophy. I have never seen a happier hunter.

Still, the question remained. Should he have killed that jake?

Of the many issues turkey hunters debate, none is more volatile than whether to shoot juvenile toms, commonly called jakes, which are usually legal targets during spring seasons.

The question is complex and includes numerous considerations.

Typically, killing jakes doesn't harm turkey populations, although wildlife agencies protect jakes in some areas because of localized population concerns. Many hunters believe killing jakes is a great way to introduce novice hunters to the sport. Also, hunters with limited time or resources often shoot jakes.

For some, however, only longbeards generate enough excitement.

The Biological Perspective

Many turkey biologists have similar opinions about the issue. Three — George Wright of Kentucky, Jack Murray of Tennessee, and Dave Baumann of South Carolina — also have another perspective. They're the primary turkey project coordinators for their states, and each has seen his state's turkey population flourish because of restoration and management programs. Also, they're avid turkey hunters.

Wright, Murray and Baumann agree there's no biological reason not to shoot jakes in most areas.

"We're conducting a telemetry study on turkeys right now and have developed some interesting data on the turkeys in our state," Wright said. "What we're discovering seems to fall in line with a study done a few years back in Missouri that indicates that we're only losing about 25 percent to 30 percent of our juvenile gobblers each year. This figure includes natural predation, hunting and poaching. Based on that data, we're having a substantial carryover of jakes into their second year.

"For mature gobblers — the 2-year-old and older birds — we're calculating that about 50 percent of these turkeys are being taken each year. Of course, because we have plenty of birds in this age class available to the hunters, it's not surprising that most hunters seem to prefer taking adult gobblers."

Wright said research indicates the mortality of gobblers excluding hunting and poaching losses is about 10 percent to 15 percent. The mortality rate of hens is about 40 percent to 60 percent. Therefore, the research indicates that killing jakes does not harm turkey populations.

Baumann concurred.

"There's simply no biological reason not to shoot a jake in South Carolina," he said. "If you have plenty of jakes, that's a good indicator that you've had a good hatch and poult survival from the previous summer. If such is the case, your population should be steady or growing. If you have a poor reproductive season, then you are much less likely to see juvenile gobblers and won't have as much opportunity to harvest them anyway.

"We're closely monitoring the number of jakes taken, and so far there's no problem in the overall number harvested. If it does become a problem, then we can take corrective action through management regulations."

In some localized cases, jakes warrant protection. However, these situations are isolated. In one state, jakes comprised about 90 percent of the harvest on public land, Wright said. Corrective regulations were enacted.

Why Some Kill Jakes

Murray said there's no scientific reason Tennessee hunters shouldn't shoot jakes. The state's turkey population is still expanding, and numerous juvenile gobblers are available to hunters in many areas. Also, he said killing jakes serves a purpose.

"I think most experienced hunters prefer longbeards, but if they're having trouble getting their first tag filled, many will probably take a jake if the opportunity arises," he said. "I hunted with a man last year who had previously killed seven elk and three bears but no turkeys. He says without question the jake he took after a wonderful hunt is the highlight of his hunting life. Without a doubt, that hunt stands as his most memorable. That jake, to that hunter, is unquestionably a trophy."

Baumann agreed.

"For youngsters or folks who haven't tried the sport before, I see no biological or other reason to hesitate to take a jake," he said.

The decision of whether to shoot a jake is often based on opportunity, Baumann said.

"Our studies in South Carolina indicate that jakes are much more likely to be harvested on public lands than on private lands," he said. "The private landowners who hunt their land probably have more opportunities to hunt, so they might pass on opportunities to take jakes more often."

"I personally would rather harvest a big ol' longbeard," Wright said. "However, I have taken jakes when the situation seemed appropriate, and I would not hesitate to have a youngster or beginning hunter with me shoot a jake. And I'll admit that when a bird comes gobbling and working my call, it's mighty tempting — even if it turns out to not be a longbeard."

Perception and Personal Views

Some hunters base their opinions on considerations other than biology and personal preference. Turkey hunting pros have developed their views through years of feedback.

Five-time world calling champion Mark Drury, a hunting video producer and founder of M.A.D. Calls, said the hunting public has a tremendous demand for adult gobblers. Drury tailors his videos to meet viewer needs, so he passes up jakes.

"The video industry is very discriminating in terms of viewership judgment," he said. "The first couple of videos we produced had two jakes taken out of about 10 birds, yet we received notable criticism from the viewing public. Our third video, *Longbeards of the Spring*, was totally dedicated to adult gobblers and received extremely favorable feedback.

"Since that time, we've produced (dozens of) feature videos, and have discovered that harvesting jakes is perfectly acceptable for youngsters. However, viewers do not want to see experienced hunters take jakes — only adult gobblers."

Drury also passes up jakes during personal hunts.

"It's a very personal decision for me," he said. "I've been fortunate to be outdoors a lot and have lots of opportunities to hunt, so I can pass up a jake with no qualms. However, I know there are a lot of hunters who do not get to hunt as much as they would like, and passing an opportunity to shoot a jake is much more difficult.

"I believe a person has to make the decision whether to harvest a jake based on the situation. You get out of the hunt what you put into it, and if that animal pleases or excites the hunter and provides the ingredients for a memorable event, then I think harvesting the young gobbler is the thing to do."

Joe Kelly, a South Carolina turkey guide, has a similar philosophy.

"The key to success is to enjoy the experience, have a good time, and take any bird that's legal and makes my client happy," Kelly said. "When a hunter has the opportunity to pursue, call to, and react to a gobbler's calls and behavior, and finally gets into position to make a clean kill, the decision of whether to harvest the bird is really moot. It's the final act of the play."

Kelly said people who don't shoot a jake because they discover at the last minute it's not a mature bird might be cheating themselves.

"If my clients decide to shoot a jake, I certainly have no qualms or (don't) think any less of them," he said. "My intent is to call in an adult bird, and that's usually what is harvested. But sometimes a jake will gobble, strut and provide the same level of excitement as any adult bird."

It's Up to You

There's no black-and-white answer to the question of whether to shoot jakes. Hunters must ask themselves what they want from a hunt, and whether that can be achieved by killing a jake. The friend I mentioned at the beginning of this story was fulfilled by his experience.

Consider the experience of your hunt, and make your choice. But be prepared to rethink your decision in the heat of the moment.

— Terry Madewell is a veteran outdoors writer from South Carolina.

CHAPTER 9

No-Name Turkeys

Bless those no-name 2-year-olds. Without them, the hunt would be an ordeal.

■ GERRY BLAIR

The turkey hunters I have known have been strange. Many of those hard hunters stay awake nights so they can ponder ways to make a difficult hunt more difficult. Most willingly hunt with a short-range getter: shotguns with ranges of two or three dozen yards — guns that demands the target be up close and personal.

There is more. Many of those strange hunters hone in on the most difficult of the difficult — street-smart birds that have earned notoriety. And if that was not enough, some extend the degree of difficulty: They set goals that involve taking birds from each of the subspecies — an effort rewarded by a sense of satisfaction and nothing more.

I consider myself as strange as the average turkey hunter. I admit to fantasies that have me hunting nonresident turkeys so I can complete the domestic and international grand slam.

Honesty makes me declare that each of those goals are, currently, unfulfilled. They might never be realized. Most of my turkey hunting has me walking familiar woods while hunting familiar birds — just like you. And most of my hunting has me marching for low-key turkeys — those I call the no-names. They're 2-year-olds; birds enjoying their first season as a 100 percent gobbler; birds that offer the main part of hunting excitement. Bless those 2-year-olds. Without them, the hunt would be an ordeal.

The no-names, as I see it, are the meat of turkey hunting. Most of the turkeys I have tagged have been no-names. Even so, being human — sort of — I often invent names for those inconspicuous gobblers so I have a call code to retrieve that memory handily. The no-name I call the Horse Biscuit Bird is an example.

I was hunting the climax ponderosa pine forest of the Navajo lands of northern Arizona when the weather turned mean. Daylight revealed 6 inches of fresh snow on the ground and more in the air.

Yep, those snowflakes were as big as horse biscuits or nearly so. I resisted the temptation to return my cold body to the warm sleeping bag. An hour later, I had parked the 4-by-4 along an Arizona freeway (a barely passable two-track).

Although I made every effort to stay discrete, the door latch of the pickup clicked as I eased the door closed. That click provoked a gobble from a bird roosted no more than a 100 yards away in the mystery of the biscuits. I walked quietly on the soft snow until I estimated I was 50 yards from the tom. I selected a setup, stayed quiet until almost flydown and offered a stingy yelp or two on my diaphragm. The bird turned insane. Double-gobble followed double-gobble — more than I cared to count. At flydown, the 2-year-old came like a 747 on IFR, almost landing in my lap.

Like most Merriam's, the bird carried stubby, ordinary spurs. The beard was likewise — thick and about 8 inches, which is typical for a 2-year-old.

Ah! No-name turkeys. I admire each of those ordinary gobblers and admire equally the ordinary hunters who hunt for them.

— *Gerry Blair is the former editor of* Turkey, The Turkey Hunter *and* Turkey & Turkey Hunting. *He lives in Arizona.*

Brian Lovett

CHAPTER 10

Eye of the Beholder: The Fallacies of Trophy Turkeys

Everyone loves to kill heavy, long-spurred gobblers. However, such features are considered after the fact. Any longbeard killed via fair chase is a trophy, whether it's 2, 3 or 4, and whether it weighs 16 or 26 pounds.

■ *BRIAN LOVETT*

R ay Eye loves to tell the story about the time he and another renowned hunter glassed a Missouri hilltop.

"There," Eye said, pointing to the crest. "Four longbeards!"

His guest took the binoculars and assessed the situation.

"They look like 2-year-olds," the man said.

Eye paused for a minute and cast a bewildered glance toward his guest before replying.

"So?"

The Misconception Factor

"So?" indeed. Eye, a renowned turkey hunter and caller who has seen hundreds of turkeys die, knows the score. Whether 2 or 5, heavy or light, limbhanger or stubby-spurred, any longbeard is a good longbeard.

But a few folks don't get it. You've probably met them: Guys who saw "three 30-pounders" the other day, or who "passed up a scrawny 2-year-old" to wait for a "better" gobbler.

Essentially, they're hunters who hold misconceptions about "trophy" turkey characteristics and, worse, insist on spouting their hogwash to anyone who will listen. Most of these guys are harmless — unless youngsters or inexperienced turkey hunters start to buy their baloney.

Then, it's time to get real.

In my opinion, any longbeard killed via fair chase is a trophy, whether it's 2, 3 or 4, and whether it weighs 16 or 26 pounds.

Some folks might disagree, and that's fine. After all, turkey hunting is an individual pursuit, and everyone's entitled to enjoy it their own way.

However, almost all experienced turkey hunters agree that there are no bad longbeards. Sure, anyone is delighted when they kill a bird with special characteristics, such as an unusual beard or long, sharp spurs, but such features are acknowledged after the fact. Video or guiding considerations aside, almost all experienced turkey nuts will greet a legal longbeard with a swarm of shot. And rightly so.

Maybe Ronnie "Cuz" Strickland, well-known turkey hunter and videographer for Mossy Oak camouflage, said it best. Years ago in Texas, he and I listened to a fellow writer who, at the urging of his guide, had let a gobbler walk because, "A bigger one would come later."

Of course, it never did. The hunter went home empty-handed from perhaps his only chance at a Rio.

Strickland smiled and shook his head.

"Who the hell passes up a longbeard?" he said.

On the Hoof

Let's get to the root of the matter. First, there is no "quality turkey management," and you can't stockpile game birds, including turkeys. A perceived 2-year-old you pass up this spring might not be around next spring.

Even if you could stockpile turkeys, it would be almost impossible to selectively kill older gobblers because it's extremely difficult to judge the age and corresponding trophy features of a live gobbler.

Turkeys don't usually provide sufficient time for a hunter to critique them. Even if they did, most judgments would be shaky — at best. Anyone who claims otherwise is full of hot air.

A gobbler's spurs provide the best gauge of its age. And trying to field-judge spurs on live turkeys — except maybe at some Texas ranches and New Zealand — is impossible. Consider this tale of woe.

Years ago, a friend was hunting with some well-known callers in Iowa. They had spotted a bird on the shoreline of a large lake and sneaked in for a closer look. The bird's chest was obscured, but its legs and head were visible.

"You can't believe the spurs on that gobbler," one caller said while looking at the bird through binoculars. "Crawl up to that little rise and shoot him."

Brian Lovett

My friend obliged, dropping the long-hooked tom on the spot. When he ran to the bird, however, it had somehow changed into a jake.

The "spurs" the caller had seen through binoculars were actually the bird's hind toes.

Really, even spur length won't definitively reveal age if a gobbler is 3 or older. In his book *After the Hunt*, Lovett E. Williams Jr. renowned turkey biologist and contributing editor for *Turkey & Turkey Hunting*, said a blunt spur that's ¾- to ⅞-inch indicates a 2-year-old gobbler, and a pointed spur slightly longer than 1 inch indicates a 3-year-old. After that, however, things get hazy.

"My observations suggest that a gobbler with a sharp, curved spur longer than 1⅛ inches is at least 3 years old, and one with a spur longer than that is probably older," he wrote. "Until more is known about spur growth, we will have to be content with separating gobblers with confidence into only three age classes according to spur length and sharpness: jake, 2-year-old and at least a 3-year-old. With somewhat less confidence, you can say that a gobbler with a sharp 1½-inch spur is probably 4 years old or older."

Remember, those numbers are from accurate measurements of dead specimens. Could someone glimpse the spur of a live gobbler and say with certainty that it was ¾ or 1¼ inches? Come on.

And beards? Don't get me started. Show me a guy who tries to field-judge turkey age by the beard, and I'll show you a guy who hasn't hunted much.

Williams said a typical 2-year-old will have a 9- to 10-inch beard that, when viewed under magnification or transmitted light, has tapered, smooth bristles and retains its original amber tips. A 3-year-old or older gobbler will typically have a 10-plus-inch beard with — again, viewed under magnification — broken, black bristle tips.

"He cannot be distinguished from older gobblers by looking at his beard," Williams wrote in *After the Hunt*.

And you can't tell me anyone could accurately field-judge a 2-year-old's beard from that of an older tom.

If you need to delude yourself, you're better off trying to check spurs.

Weight a Minute

Many guys base their field judgments on size. Everyone has seen strutters that appear huge, but good luck guessing their weight. Typically, you cannot do it accurately. Remember, a gobbler's spring weight depends greatly on the fat in its breast sponge, and you can't gauge that till you skin a bird. Therefore, turkeys might look identical but vary greatly in weight.

One spring in Missouri, three-time world-champion caller Don Shipp and I doubled a pair of hot-gobbling longbeards. The toms looked like twins in every respect. But at the registration station, Shipp's bird weighed 23 pounds and mine weighed 17. Had my bird bred hens that spring, thereby losing weight, while his buddy looked on? Perhaps, but who knows?

In addition, it's often difficult to put a turkey's size in perspective, because most strutting gobblers appear huge. Years ago in the Ozarks, I watched Gregg and Tom Neumann of Penn's Woods Calls kill two gorgeous strutting toms — the kind that look like giant black puffballs pirouetting across a pasture. The earth seemed to tremble as the heavyweights slowly worked to the gun, and everyone who witnessed the hunt commented on the "big turkeys."

They weighed 15½ and 16½ pounds.

Sometimes, you might gauge a turkey's relative size, like when one gobbler towers over nearby longbeards. No doubt, that's a big turkey, but how big? You only know that it's larger than its peers. It might look like a mythical 30-pounder next to smaller gobblers, but that would only be a guess. Williams said many of those "30-pounders" tend to shrink when placed on certified scales.

Actually, Williams believes weight is even a dubious post-mortem trophy feature. He said there's a poor correlation between weight and wariness, and even weight and age past about age 2. Further, a turkey's weight will vary greatly during the year, and from year to year. It will even vary daily. Also, a gobbler will always be heavier in spring than fall.

So, if you'll pardon the pun, size holds little weight.

Brian Lovett

The Essence of Turkey Hunting

OK, let's forget the myth of field-judging and examine philosophy.

Why anyone would attempt to field-judge a gobbler is beyond me. Turkey hunting isn't about the size of the quarry. All longbeards are relatively similar physically, and again, that's an after-the-kill consideration. The important thing is that longbeards gobble, strut, drum and act like the perplexing, mystifying critters they are. They send shivers up your spine, thrill you with unmatched interaction and seem to frustrate you at every turn.

Really, that's what turkey hunting is about: the hunt; pitting your knowledge and experience against a gobbler's evolution-honed survival instincts. It's about calling, maneuvering and the continuing chess game between you and a bird. It's equal parts preparation, perseverance and prognostication. And it hasn't changed much since American Indians yelped through handmade wingbones and wielded wooden bows and arrows.

From a challenge standpoint, a turkey hunter must be complete: a knowledgeable, experienced woodsman who can call and anticipate a turkey's next move. Further, he must use those skills for every bird, regardless of its age. Sure, many older gobblers act differently than their younger compatriots. However, I've seen razor-hooked old-timers almost trip over their beards running to calling, yet I've watched dull-spurred 2-year-olds — and sometimes jakes — frustrate hunters for days by playing hard to get. You never know how the game will play out, and you must be ready for anything.

Again, it's about the pursuit, not a bird's physical attributes. Remember what a veteran Alabama turkey guru told me years ago: "When you kill a turkey, you're basically left with a pile of meat and feathers. It's what goes into killing that turkey that makes it memorable."

Amen.

Trophies of the Mind

I've been fortunate to shoot some heavy, long-spurred gobblers, all of which I cherish. But one nondescript longbeard stands above all others.

It was May 2000, and I had just returned to Wisconsin from several weeks of hunting out of state. I had two-and-a-half days to hunt at home before family obligations and another trip ended my home-state season.

I hadn't been able to scout much, and the first two days were a bust. I worked a gobbler at daylight the third day, but he wandered off with a hen and eventually shut up. Soon, I hit the road and began calling at various spots. By 11 a.m., I had netted nothing. Worse, the sun was baking the landscape, sending temperatures soaring toward 90.

"One more hour to hunt," I thought. "I'm sunk."

Having no other options, I returned to where I'd worked the bird that morning. I slipped into some pines and offered a few yelps and cutts. Silence. I repeated the sequence again. Nothing.

I slumped against a tree and accepted my fate. Skunked.

Just then, however, a crow flew over a small hardwood glade about 150 yards away. His raucous "caw-caw-caws" echoed across the farm-country landscape.

"Gaaaarrrrrrrrrrrrrobbbbbbbbbbble!"

That rat! He was still there, probably loafing in the shade with the hen.

I raced out of the pines and crept up a fence line toward the oaks. Quietly, I slipped to one side of the patch and offered some light clucks. The hen clucked back about 60 yards away, but the gobbler remained silent and invisible.

After about 10 minutes, I knew I had to force the issue. I crawled to the other end of the glade, slipped out of my vest and began crawling toward the trees, calling as I went.

Soon, movement caught my eye. Gobbler!

The bird rubber-necked left to right, searching for that "other hen." I froze, praying the grassy hill behind me would conceal my obvious form. The bird eyed me suspiciously, and then turned back toward the trees. I was about to cluck when he stopped and raised his head high for one final look.

I barely remember the shot or the sprint to the downed bird. But I remember hoisting him over my shoulder and grinning all the way to the truck. I'd plucked victory from certain defeat, killing a longbeard with less than five minutes to hunt.

Forever a Trophy

The trophy stats of that 2-year-old were nothing special. Weight unknown; beard, 9-some inches; spurs, ¼-inch and stubby.

And in my book, he'll always be No. 1.

— *Brian Lovett served as editor of* Turkey & Turkey Hunting *from August 1995 through January 2002. He hails from central Wisconsin.*

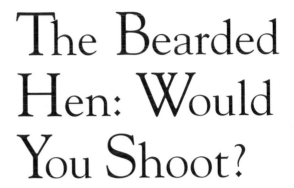

CHAPTER 11

The Bearded Hen: Would You Shoot?

Many hunters would never consider killing a bearded hen during spring, even if it's legal. Other folks, however, consider bearded hens fair game.

■ *JOHN TROUT JR.*

I could barely see the wooded Missouri ravine in the early-morning light. Nestled between two pastures, however, I easily heard two gobblers that serenaded the valley 200 yards from the small oak I sat against.

Surprise, Surprise

When dawn arrived, my turkey talk convinced the gobblers to leave the roost and investigate the "hen" they heard. The longbeards slowly strutted into the pasture, determined to close the distance between us. My gun was already shouldered when the birds stopped and began gobbling 50 yards from me. It seemed I would be squeezing the trigger within moments. Then, trouble arrived.

After hearing rustling leaves to my right, I scanned the area, expecting to see another tom sneaking in. A few frantic heartbeats later, I spotted the new arrival 25 yards away. I also saw a slender beard swinging with every step the turkey took, but I knew this bird didn't resemble a gobbler. It was a bearded hen, walking toward the gobblers, which stood and gazed at her approach.

If the gobblers had been out of view, I would have frightened the hen away before she reached them. However, I could do nothing to change the outcome of the hunt. The hen walked to the strutting longbeards and led them back into the wooded ravine. Meanwhile, I called in vain.

That incident occurred in the early 1980s. The bearded hen was legal game, but I never considered shooting her. Since then, I have encountered three other bearded hens while hunting.

I have never killed a bearded hen. Other hunters, though, consider bearded hens fair game during spring.

Examining the Odd Lady

In *The Book of the Wild Turkey*, Lovett E. Williams Jr. wrote that beards occur more frequently in domestic hens than wild hens. Also, he said hen beards rarely exceed 8 inches and are thinner than gobbler beards.

Other turkey abnormalities probably occur less frequently than hen beards. I've only seen four bearded hens while hunting during the past 20 years. However, I photograph turkeys about 60 days every spring, and I usually see at least one bearded hen out of the 20 or 30 hens I view. I've also seen off-colored turkeys, mature gobblers without beards, gobblers with multiple beards and mature gobblers without spurs. However, I see many more bearded hens than birds with other abnormalities.

It's not clear how many hens have beards. Bob Eriksen, New Jersey's wild turkey biologist, said his state has trapped 1,560 turkeys since 1978, of which 979 were hens. Of the 979 hens, 77, or about 7.87 percent, had beards. However, Eriksen said that might be misleading, because the beards of juvenile hens might not be noticeable. Eriksen said out of the 547 adult hens trapped, 71, or about 12.98 percent, had beards. Of the 432 juveniles trapped, six, or about 1.39 percent, had noticeable beards.

New Jersey has released turkeys at about 39 sites in 16 counties, and has released at least one bearded hen at every site. However, Eriksen said the bearded hen releases weren't intentional.

Shoot or Pass?

You can legally kill bearded hens in many states during spring. These states seem to write regulations so no bearded turkey is protected. For example, Indiana regulations state hunters can kill, "One bearded or male turkey per season." Other states have similar regulations. The 1997 Illinois Digest of Hunting and Trapping Regulations said: "It is unlawful to take a wild turkey, except a gobbler (male), or a hen with a visible beard."

These regulations are designed to make hunters identify beards before shooting. Steve Backs, an Indiana wild turkey biologist, said many states have laws about bearded turkeys to prevent perplexing situations.

"The beard is a typical mark, and about 95 percent of the time, it depicts a male turkey," he said. "If we tried to go to another regulation that didn't tell hunters to look for a bearded turkey, it could create confusion."

Safety is the No. 1 objective of beard regulations. The only other rule option is to ask hunters to identify the colors of a gobbler, especially its red, white and blue head. Some officials fear this rule could be unsafe, because more hunters might be mistaken for turkeys. If hunters must look for beards, they're less likely to shoot at something that's red, white or blue. However, Backs said there's a flip-side to this theory.

"Some say that if a hunter has to look for only a beard, they're more apt to shoot at somebody's gun strap," he said.

What do You Look For?

I seldom look for a beard unless I'm attempting to distinguish jakes from longbeards. It can be difficult to see a beard, especially when a gobbler struts and faces a hunter. I usually see a tom's beard, but I identify turkeys by the colors of their heads and bodies. A jake's head colors don't always closely resemble those of a longbeard or a hen.

Like most hunters, I'm confident I'll never mistake a hen for a gobbler. I mistook a jake for a longbeard once, but I've never mistaken a tom for a hen. I'm certain I'll never think a hen is a gobbler, even if she has a beard.

Although regulations tell hunters to look for beards, hunters should also identify turkeys by their size, color and head colors. A hen might have a beard, but it won't have the size and colors of a tom.

This leads to the real question: Should a hunter knowingly shoot a bearded hen if it's legal?

I have no desire to kill a bearded hen. I turkey hunt because I want to call a gobbler into range. A bearded hen that happens by doesn't fit my plans, and I don't consider killing one a challenge.

Also, regulations protect hens during spring so hens can raise more turkeys for future seasons. Bearded hens have no reproductive abnormalities. They can incubate clutches and raise poults like other hens.

Many hunters who kill bearded hens have reasons for doing so. Some have shot bearded hens because the birds are unusual. Others want bearded hens for trophies. I'd rather hear about a hunter shooting a bearded hen for those reasons. I have a problem with hunters who shoot bearded hens because they mistook them for gobblers. Guys who claim they killed bearded hens because they saw beards didn't identify their targets before shooting.

Illegal or Accidental Harvest

I believe some bearded hens are shot by people who just want to illegally kill hens. However, after they discover the hen has a beard, they realize they have a legal turkey.

No one knows how many bearded hens hunters kill. In some states where hunters must register birds, registration forms don't specify a bird's sex.

Some officials don't believe hunters kill many bearded hens in spring.

"I don't see the number of bearded hens shot as an impact on the turkey population," Backs said.

However, Backs believes illegal hen harvest could affect the flock. Many hens are killed accidentally because hunters hear toms gobble, and then shoot at the first movement that looks like a turkey.

New Jersey limits hunters to gobblers only. According to Eriksen, these regulations are designed to protect hens and make hunters safety conscious.

"Our intent is to protect hens, but the other side of the regulations is to force turkey hunters to spend some time learning to distinguish between toms and hens using attributes other than the beard," he said. "This makes them look for head, neck and breast coloration, the size of the turkey and the beard. This regulation actually makes the hunter look for more than one physical characteristic to make this determination."

Eriksen said most hens killed illegally in New Jersey don't have beards. Also, he said that during the past 17 seasons, New Jersey has had only five hunting accidents. However, he attributed the record to the state's permit system as much as the gobbler-only rule. He claimed the permit system reduces hunter densities and interactions.

Conclusion

The bearded hen dilemma boils down to this: States that let hunters kill bearded hens do so because of identification factors, not so hunters can have additional targets. Nonetheless, in these states, killing bearded hens is legal.

I don't consider a bearded hen more desirable than any other hen during spring. However, another hunter might want to shoot a bearded hen because it's unusual. I respect this.

I enjoy watching bearded hens, but they're just like other hens. Given a chance, they'll run off with the gobbler you were about to kill.

— John Trout Jr. is an accomplished turkey and deer hunter from southern Indiana.

CHAPTER 12

Let's Expand Fall Hunting

Maybe soon, we can view fall turkey hunting as a widespread part of the American hunting scene.

■ JIM CASADA

There's no debate the widespread introduction of spring gobbler hunting is the critical element in the turkey's great comeback. Every hunter who has been thrilled by a gobble at daybreak can be thankful, and biologists and other stewards who contributed to the resurgence deserve credit.

However, many biologists and hunters overlook another facet of the sport — fall turkey hunting. In fact, many of them are against fall turkey seasons.

I believe they're mistaken. What follows is an argument for at least a partial return to turkey hunting's roots.

The Biology

Wildlife biologists have divided opinions about fall hunting. Some authorities believe fall hunting, under proper guidelines, makes sense. Others don't want fall hunts, and argue that spring hunting is almost the only reason turkey numbers are at all-time highs.

However, the real question is: "Can you have fall hunting and sustain sound turkey populations?" After all, state biologists have two duties: The foremost is to protect and sustain the resource. The second — one that's being ignored in many cases regarding fall seasons — is to hunters.

If turkey populations can thrive with fall hunting, autumn seasons should be allowed — period. When wildlife authorities don't allow fall hunting during these circumstances, they're not fulfilling their duties to the folks who pay their salaries — hunters.

Most arguments against fall hunting — at least in areas where turkey restorations are complete — are specious. My home state, South Carolina, is a good example. Several years ago, South Carolina abandoned a week-long fall season held in parts of the state. Biologists argued — correctly — that several consecutive poor hatches necessitated the closure. However, when the season was discontinued, there was an implicit promise that fall hunting would be restored after several good hatches increased turkey numbers.

The good hatches occurred, but South Carolina still doesn't have a fall season.

However, you can kill a whopping five gobblers during spring in the state. Further, the answers hunters receive when they ask about resuming fall hunting don't deal with turkey populations.

The Reasons?

Officials don't discuss the heart of the matter.

They say fall turkey hunters might have conflicts with deer hunters, although the 1997 deer season — in one form or another — will run for 3½ months in the areas where fall hunting was legal. Also, officials allude to overharvest caused by fall hunting years ago. However, at one time, fall hunters could kill 15 birds per season, and the season ran from early autumn through Feb. 28. Further, officials overlook or have forgotten the real question: Is fall hunting biologically viable?

It is, without question, in South Carolina and many states where restoration efforts are complete. In such situations, fall hunting should be allowed.

Similar situations exist in many states. Concerned hunters come to an obvious but unacceptable conclusion: Officials are captives of a spring-only mentality. They ignore reality, or simply like to boast about record numbers of birds while ignoring fall hunting's feasibility.

After a spring-only mind set is entrenched, it's difficult to dislodge. It happened with the "bucks-only" attitude among deer hunters. Many old-timers refuse to shoot does but will kill spikes. Likewise, the biological reasons for limiting spring turkey hunting to half days are obsolete, but many states still hold half-day spring hunts.

How Fall Seasons Can Work

Maybe it's better to look at fall hunting success stories.

Virginia is a prime example. The state has a long tradition of fall hunting, including the use of dogs. Also, Virginia has avoided potential conflicts between deer hunters and turkey hunters by adjusting seasons. Turkeys are faring well in Virginia, which proves fall hunting is viable.

Lovett E. Williams Jr., a wildlife biologist and contributing editor for *Turkey & Turkey Hunting*, who is recognized as the country's leading turkey authority, offered another perspective on fall hunting.

"I think fall hunting is the best, and biologically it can certainly be justified," he said. "Unfortunately, the current trend seems to be away from fall hunting, and to me that is a shame. After all, hunting during this season provides a much greater opportunity for real interaction with turkeys. In fall, you can have real discourse and hear a great deal from turkeys, much more so than is the case in spring."

Jim Schlender

Williams' thoughts make a concise, compelling case for expanding fall hunting. They're also a reminder — for hunters who believe hearing a tom gobble is the ultimate thrill — that you can have "conversations" with turkeys during fall.

Should Hens Be Protected?

Some people argue against fall hunting because they believe too many hens and poults are killed during fall seasons. Admittedly, the easiest birds to kill during fall are from flocks — most often hens and poults — that have been broken up and called back. However, in areas with good turkey populations, killing hens and poults in reasonable numbers isn't a problem. The harvest can be controlled by seasonal limits.

Overly cautious officials could at least allow fall gobbler hunting. Alabama does this. It takes savvy to distinguish an immature jake in fall, but it can be done, and hunters can benefit from this learning experience.

As another alternative, serious hunters might shoot only longbeards in fall. Henry Edwards Davis, whose book *The American Wild Turkey* is the finest work ever published on the sport, once suggested any fool could kill a lovesick spring gobbler.

However, Edwards said, to call in and kill a mature tom during fall is turkey hunting's crowning achievement. It's difficult to argue.

A Sense of Tradition

Mentioning Davis and other hunters from yesteryear brings up another argument for fall hunting — tradition.

Most modern hunters are ignorant of this. I believe less than 10 percent of today's turkey hunters are intimately familiar with fall hunting. They dismiss it as "too easy," or offer opinions like, "I don't want to hunt 'em unless I hear them gobble." However, the same hunters — probably to a man — would pull the trigger without thinking twice if a spring gobbler came in silently.

Those who cherish fall hunting know it has its own appeal — one that's distinct from spring hunting. Hunters must use different attributes of woodsmanship, calling and set-up techniques. The nature of the quarry is different.

Tradition and the sport's roots shouldn't be overlooked. Historians have said, "You can't know where you're going if you don't know where you've been." Too few turkey hunters know where their sport has been, and that's sad. If they read books by the sport's old masters — men such as Davis, Archibald Rutledge, Simon Everitt, E.A. McIlhenny and Tom Turpin — they would discover a little-known facet of

---

The Arguments for Expanding Fall Hunting

- The sport's traditions focus on fall hunting.
- In many areas where restoration efforts are complete and turkeys are faring well, fall hunting is biologically viable.
- Fall hunting provides sportsmen with new experiences.
- Fall hunting offers special challenges and perspectives.
- Fall seasons give hunters a wider view of the turkey's world.
- Wildlife officials have a duty to hunters — one that's currently unfulfilled in many areas — to provide them with hunting opportunities if the resource allows.

In many areas, turkey populations could withstand the added pressure of fall hunting.

Jim Casada

---

the sport and would likely develop a greater appreciation for fall hunting.

Conclusion

Fall turkey hunting isn't for everyone, and I don't want to dictate hunters' tastes. Still, there's truth in the words, "don't knock it until you've tried it."

If the resource is available, fall hunting is biologically viable, and fall seasons are working in several states, why not allow fall hunting? It would open new horizons, provide hunters with a link to their roots, and increase the number of days hunters could match wits with turkeys.

States, including those that don't currently have fall seasons, can attain these benefits without hurting the resource. In areas where turkey numbers don't justify two-season hunting, officials should set fall hunting as a management goal.

Then maybe, not long from now, we can view fall turkey hunting as a widespread part of the American hunting scene.

— Jim Casada served as co-editor of Turkey & Turkey Hunting *for several years, and is currently the magazine's editor-at-large. He hails from Rock Hill, S.C.*

CHAPTER 13

What of the Future?

Most wildlife professionals are cautiously optimistic about the turkey's future, but two of the country's top turkey biologists disagree about what the 21st century will hold.

■ BRIAN LOVETT

As you take a minute to slap yourself on the back, think about the future. Here's what we know: Thanks to hunters, volunteers, biologists, state and federal wildlife agencies, and private conservation groups — especially the National Wild Turkey Federation — turkeys and turkey hunting are flourishing. America has more than 5 million turkeys and 2.5 million turkey hunters.

But what about the 21st century? That depends who you ask. Most wildlife professionals are cautiously optimistic, but two of the country's top turkey biologists disagree about what the future will hold.

The Good

"I'm very optimistic for several reasons," said Lovett E. Williams Jr., one of the country's best-known turkey biologists and contributing editor to *Turkey & Turkey Hunting.*

"The turkey is well adapted to a much broader range of habitat conditions than we ever thought before. It's also more compatible with a human presence than we ever thought. We're seeing that when people don't shoot hens and poults, turkeys are everywhere."

Williams also believes turkey hunting has a great future, thanks mostly to the sport's unique appeal.

"Hunters are satisfied without killing a whole lot of animals," he said. "Quail hunting is hopeless. Duck hunting will one day go down the drain. But a turkey hunter can go out and be unsuccessful day after day, and it doesn't dampen his zeal for turkey hunting. Then, when he kills one, he's successful. It has that going for it, and other kinds of hunting don't.

"Turkey hunting has changed from being not much different than squirrel hunting or duck hunting ... into a stylized type of hunting. People are basically accepting a kind of ethic and are adopting many of the same ideals."

Williams acknowledges that booming turkey numbers lead to increasing hunter numbers and pressure. However, he doesn't think that will cause problems.

"I think even with more turkey hunting pressure — which I think we'll see more of, because it's a great bird to hunt — I think turkeys can handle that," he said. "Also, agencies can regulate turkey hunting better than many other things."

In fact, Williams expects turkey hunting to thrive and, perhaps, outlive similar pursuits.

"I think it might be one of the last game birds that's ever hunted successfully in a long-term tradition," he said. "I think the future is very good."

The Bad

George Hurst, former professor of wildlife management at Mississippi State University, foresees a different future for turkeys and turkey hunters — at least in the Southeast.

Hurst said the South's turkey population explosion is finished. Typically, bird populations boom and peak several years after restoration is complete. Then, turkey numbers subside and stabilize.

Also, Hurst believes urban sprawl, an increasing human population and modern forestry practices will decrease and degrade turkey habitat throughout much of the prime Southern turkey range.

"We (turkey hunters) are a tiny minority when it comes to land use," he said. "I'm looking at 5 million acres of the Mississippi Delta, the most productive soil in the country. What is it devoted to, and what will it be even more devoted to? Production of food and fiber for man. Period. End of discussion."

Hurst cited heavy timber harvests in states such as Alabama, Mississippi and Louisiana as prime examples.

"The South's future has to be negative, because forest products are the No. 1 crop," he said. "We're the wood basket of the nation, if you know what that means."

Trees are renewable resources, but Hurst said the short-rotation pine plantations that typically replace mixed mature hardwood/pine forests make poor turkey habitat.

Many forests are cut every 15 to 20 years, and managers don't conduct any prescribed burns on these areas, Hurst said.

"Those pine plantations are not anywhere near the quality of habitat as a 60-year-old pine plantation that's burned every three to four years," he said.

"A turkey says, 'You took my mature forest, which produces mast, and gave me this damn thing?'"

Modern forestry practices also fragment areas of mature forests, which adds to another problem — predation.

"The old-forest fragmentation is a thing of the deep South," Hurst said. "It increases patchiness, which is great for predators and disaster for turkeys. All the damn land use favors predation.

"It produces a real high prey base for feral dogs, coyotes, bobcats, hogs, owls and snakes, and makes great food sources for raccoons, possums and skunks. Wait a minute. The turkey loses; predators win."

Hurst also lamented urban sprawl in many areas, notably Georgia and Florida.

Biologists, hunters, conservation groups, hunting clubs and some other private landowners will do their part to maintain turkey habitat and numbers, Hurst said. However, it's unlikely they can gain ground against the current trends.

As that occurs, Hurst said, the number of turkey hunters will likely decrease, which spells more bad news for turkeys.

"The turkey will lose avid friends," he said. "That hurts. I lost a guy who used to go to meetings, speak out for turkeys and spend a fortune to turkey hunt. He's now buying golf clubs and all that other stuff."

The Truth?

Depending who you believe, the turkey's future is bright or bleak. That scenario will likely play out during the next century.

It's difficult to believe a bird that has made such a comeback and inspires millions of followers could fall on difficult times again — even if some signs point that way.

— Brian Lovett served as editor of Turkey & Turkey Hunting *from August 1995 through January 2002. Currently, he is the editor of* Bass Pro Shops' Outdoor World *magazine.*

NWTF Paves the Way for Turkey Restoration

It's difficult to imagine the modern turkey hunting scene without the National Wild Turkey Federation.

Then again, without the NWTF, the current turkey boom might never have happened.

Thanks to its grass-roots approach, thousands of volunteers and forward-looking vision, the group has championed and enabled America's greatest conservation success story — the comeback of the wild turkey.

And believe it or not, the NWTF has set its sights higher.

Starting Small, Growing Quickly

In the early 1970s, Thomas F. Rodgers, an insurance manager and outdoor writer for the *Free Lance Star* in Fredericksburg, Va., had an idea. Disturbed by threats to turkey habitat in northern Virginia, Rodgers wanted to create a group to benefit the wild turkey. He talked about his concept with hunters, biologists and call-makers, and on March 28, 1973, chartered the NWTF. The group's stated goal was to protect and enhance the habitat of the wild turkey.

At that time, America had just 1.3 million wild turkeys and 1.5 million turkey hunters.

By the end of 1973, the group had moved from Fredericksburg, Va., to Edgefield, S.C., and had conceived *Turkey Call* magazine. The NWTF boasted a membership of 1,200 volunteers who had raised about $15,000.

The NWTF was set up as a volunteer, grass-roots group governed by a board of directors. Volunteers are organized in state and local chapters. South Carolina became the first state chapter in 1974, and Georgia and Kentucky received charters later that year.

As the group grew, its efforts gained steam. The NWTF held its first national convention Feb. 4 and 5, 1977, in Hershey, Pa., and Terry Rohm won the first Grand National calling contest.

Also in 1977, the NWTF awarded its first grant for wild turkey research: $2,900 to biologist Bill Healy with the U.S. Forest Service in Morgantown, W.Va., to examine turkey production, poult survival and habitat use.

In 1980, the group broke ground for its Wild Turkey Center in Edgefield.

In 1981, the NWTF established its Juniors Acquiring Knowledge, Ethics and Sportsmanship, or JAKES, program. The effort is designed to inform, educate and involve youths 17 and younger in wildlife conservation and natural resources stewardship.

In March 1981, Rodgers resigned as the NWTF's executive vice president and was replaced by Rob Keck, who had served previously as the group's director of chapter development. Keck, a former teacher and turkey calling champion from Pennsylvania, has led the NWTF since.

Really Rolling

In 1985, the group established its Wild Turkey Super Fund, which pays for NWTF's conservation and education programs. It pools money raised at Super Fund membership banquets. Through the fund, more than $100 million has been spent on almost 10,000 projects, including education, restoration, research, equipment, law-enforcement, land acquisition and hunter's safety.

Also in 1985, the NWTF started its Making Tracks partnership with the U.S. Forest Service. The cooperative effort is designed to help pay for habitat projects and educational activities on national forest lands. The program has spent about $5.2 million on about 700 projects in 38 states.

In 1987, the NWTF released the first wild turkey under its Target 2000 program. Target 2000 is a cooperative initiative between the NWTF and state and federal wildlife agencies to restore turkeys to all remaining unoccupied habitat by 2000. To date, the group has supplied agencies with more than 105,000 turkey transport boxes, which have helped move more than 150,000 birds.

By 1993, the NWTF had more than 500 state and local chapters. Also that year, the group began its Hunting Heritage Program, which supports groups involved in hunting advocacy and traditional wildlife management.

In 1995, NWTF boasted more than 100,000 members. By 1998, the group had more than 180,000 members and more than 1,000 chapters. Also that year, the group printed its 100,000th turkey transport box, and the Target 2000 program had relocated more than 10,000 turkeys.

Success and Beyond

By 2003, the NWTF's success was no secret. Thanks in large part to the group's efforts, America had about 5.6 million turkeys — 4.3 million more than when the group started — and about 2.6 million turkey hunters. Forty-nine states and parts of Canada feature turkey hunting. Alaska, which is too far north to support turkeys, is the lone exception.

As of 2003, the NWTF had about 450,000 members in every state, Canada and 11 other countries. Also, it had about 176,000 JAKES members, 43,000 Women in the Outdoors program members, 8,000 Wheelin' Sportsman members and almost 2,000 chapters.

The group produces numerous publications, including *Turkey Call, The Caller, JAKES Magazine, Wheelin' Sportsmen* and *Women in the Outdoors*. Also, it produces *Turkey Call* and *Turkey Country* television programs.

The NWTF entered the 21st century with a full head of steam, which can only be good news for turkeys.

— *Brian Lovett*

THE MAGNIFICENT OBSESSION

I doubt I'll offend you when I say that turkey hunters are bonkers. Argue if you want, but you know it's true.

We practice the obviously irrational while never questioning our motivation or reward. We set alarms for 2 a.m. without blinking, sit and crawl in the mud and brambles without hesitation, and even drive hellbent from state to state to wrangle a few more days of hunting.

But you know that. Heck, you're dreaming about and planning for it right now. So what follows won't look at why turkey hunters are so passionate. Rather, it simply pays homage to that and looks at various facets of the obsession.

This section examines our ethics and actions afield. It reveals glimpses of the thought and anticipation we give to turkey hunting. And it shares tales of the success and ever-present failures that are such large parts of the sport.

So basically, it covers familiar territory. You'll likely relate to much of the debate and shared misfortune in the stories to come.

And sometimes, it's just nice to know that other folks share your passion in the magnificent obsession.

■ BRIAN LOVETT

I Believe

I'm wide awake and ready to play my part in the drama of the big woods. The only thing missing is the gobbler. But I'm not worried. I believe.

■ JOEL SPRING

The sun hasn't cleared the horizon yet, and has barely begun to change the woods from black to gray when I hear the first gobble. The call seems to come from the hemlock valley below me, but as has been proven many times in these echoing hills, it's almost impossible to discern the origin of a single, distant sound.

How many times had I thought one of my hunting partners had shot only to find empty hands at the end of the day? And how many times through the years had someone met me with a big tom or a nice white-tailed buck when I'd never heard their shot? These questions are among the many blurry, disjointed things that rattle in my groggy mind before the sun warms the hillside. I nestle back against the fallen white birch trunk, snug in the center of the blowdown and await legal daylight. In the shadow of the hills, that has little to do with actual daylight.

Ten minutes to go.

Brian Lovett

The Great Divide

I am awakened almost 20 minutes later by another gobble. This one is much closer than the first, and it definitely originated from the hemlock valley. I curse myself for falling asleep. I knew I should have had that other cup of coffee.

I'm sitting on top of the steep hill, but my view into the valley is obstructed by an ancient stone fence. Twenty yards to my left, there's a 3-foot-wide opening in the 4-foot-high wall. This is the only break in 200 yards of fence. It's the perfect ambush spot. I've sat in this spot countless times before, armed with various equipment. Whatever tool I've held across my lap — rifle, bow, camera or the old beat-up pump shotgun I hold this morning — I've rarely been disappointed. I wish I could recall how many times deer and turkeys had appeared here and crossed the wall, passing within feet of me.

I strain to see beyond the opening, but it's useless. The hill drops too sharply. The old fence is a divider in many respects. It divides the "upper side" from "down below," as they're called during deer season. It divides the mature beeches from the birch blowdowns. It divides civilization from the woods. And it divides here from there.

Today, it only divides me from the noisy tom below.

Visitors

Wondering how close the turkey is, I carefully pick up the call and produce a series of soft clucks. There's a long, almost contemplative silence, and then a tom below me double-gobbles while a hen behind me lets loose a long, low purr. I almost leap from the blind in surprise.

I slowly turn and spot the hen 50 yards behind me. I put my call down, hoping the hen will do all the work. She purrs a couple of more times behind me, and I hear her scratching steps approaching. She's close enough that I can hear the brittle sound of ruffling feathers.

The most direct route from the gobbler to the hen is right past my blind. I hold my breath and try to release it gently. My job is to stay still while she leads in the tom. Hopefully, he'll walk up to find her, not vice versa.

The tom lets out a hopeful gobble from below, but it isn't answered. Suddenly, two heads appear in the fence opening. They're hens. I look down, trying to avoid eye contact with the birds, which aren't quite 20 yards from me. I spy on them from under the bill of my cap. They look back and forth across the fence opening and in my direction. Their heads bob, weave and tilt in that unnerving way turkey hunters know well. They're looking at me. No, they're not.

Brian Lovett

I'm relieved when they finally pass the blind, ignoring the hen decoy between us. I hear a slight disturbance and some quiet purring behind me, so I guess they have hooked up with the first hen. I'm hoping the gobbler will be along behind them. I tighten my grip on the weathered shotgun and touch the safety button with my fingertip, as if it will help.

There He Is

Suddenly, the tom appears broadside in the opening for a second or two. He's in full strut, and his long beard is proudly displayed. It's an incredibly easy shot, but there's no time to raise the shotgun. In an instant, he's gone again. I hear him walking behind the protective curtain of stone between us, and feel my heart pounding.

The sun has risen and it warms the hilltop. The hens purr and cluck quietly behind me, more excited than before. They're oblivious to any danger I present, but they seem anxious for the appearance of the tom. They're not the only ones. I'm wide awake and ready to play my part in the drama of the big woods. The only thing missing is the gobbler. But

I'm not worried. I believe he'll come through the opening to my side of the fence.

I believe it as strongly as I believe that this afternoon, a brown trout will fall for a hook dressed with feathers from last fall's tom when the fly is drifted over an old familiar stream. I believe it like I believed the sun would rise on my cold bones this early May morning. I believe it the way I believed many years ago that a buck would cross this same opening during opening day of my first deer hunt. I believe it as much as I believe the old stone wall will still be here 100 years from now, long after my last hunt.

Conclusion

I hear scratchy footfalls approaching the opening. Behind the ancient stone wall, I can barely see the blue on top of the huge bird's head.

I believe.

— *Joel Spring is a hunter, angler and writer from New York.*

CHAPTER 2

Birds of the Mind

Turkey hunting pits human thought vs. a bird's well-honed paranoia.

■ JOE ARNETTE

Turkeys require thought. Indeed, everything about them demands attention. They are not casual birds and, likewise, they are not for casual hunters. Nor are they for shooters. Doves are for those of us who like to pull the trigger; turkeys are not. Mostly, what we do with a turkey gun is load it, carry it, sit with it and unload it.

Turkey hunting is measured in patience and hours. Turkey shooting, when it occurs, is a matter of deliberation and seconds. Turkey hunting involves more intellect than luck, more motion than productivity, more reaction than action and more life than death.

Turkeys are birds of the mind. They are wild birds not only of the edge, but on the edge. Their hair-trigger nerves are laced with paranoia, a deep suspicion of every movement and sound not of their own making. All of which means that turkey hunting is a tactical exercise comprising much more than occasional upland ramblings.

Serious turkey hunters are perfectionists at the top of their game. The birds they pursue beneath the grandeur of new days will remain forever wild. Come spring, the quest for this wildness is a better reason than most to watch a dawn break. Yet, nowhere in codes of personal conduct is it written that this experience must be defined by a dead turkey.

From another angle, turkeys force us to consider where we are. The rising sun that adds its glistening touch to dew-laden spiderwebs and warms the emerging green of youthful ferns is also part of the hunt. To not pause and take notice

Brian Lovett

of these things is to lose a bit of the bird's magic; of how and where it lives.

A Familiar Hunt

Sharply angled sunlight streamed through the birches. It danced on limbs before ricocheting off snowy-white bark and settling on last year's fallen leaves.

At the edge of the birch stand, the creamy whiteness was thinned by upright ranks of aspen-gray and scattered triangles of pine-green. This in turn faded downward into a rich-emerald sprawl of blackberry brambles. Here a soft breeze rustled in harmony with the sliding murmur of the creek that threaded its way toward the river's shallow backwater.

A great blue heron stood in the slack water, seemingly tethered to its own hazy reflection. It turned its head at a quickening of the downsloping air, listened, then cut its bond with the water, lifting across the river to safety.

The heron made its ungainly landing at the same moment a man eased through the woods upslope. Camouflage showed between the trees in wisps, revealed only by its movement. The man wearing the camo stopped, edged backward to stand tight against the trunk of a lone oak tree far from the water's edge and waited for the woods to settle.

The man had hunted this large sweep of cover for more than a decade, and he paused at the oak each time he worked the area. He stood quietly, head up, predator-like, as if subtly assessing wind, moisture, hints of noise. In reality, he was pondering exactly what the turkey he had been following — and playing games with — since dawn would do in the next moment. Or in the next hour.

Skill vs. Paranoia

It was the hunter's business to trick the turkey into range. Conversely, it was the bird's business to outwit the hunter. At its simplest, it was a question of whether skill, experience and thought could overcome innate paranoia, which held the home-field advantage.

Brian Lovett

The man yelped softly several times, waited a half-minute, then called again. Silence. He thought the bird was losing interest and moving off, angling upward from the creek toward the oak plateau above the birch stand. He believed he had nothing to lose, so he ripped loud, aggressive runs from the box call. The gobbler answered like he owned the woods, but refused to close on the sounds.

The man slipped away from the oak, worked up the slope, skirted the dense berry brambles and blended into the aspen clusters. He weaved between short pines and, for an instant, saw the turkey's head bob above a jumble of scrub growth. The bird stared narrow-eyed at him 50 yards ahead in an open, sunny glade. Then, the bird was gone as quickly as it had appeared.

The man crouched and took three steps to the side, focusing on where the bird had been. He glimpsed a metallic flash, not to his front where the gobbler should have been, but well off to the side, screened by the line of pines he had just passed. Then the turkey was gone, screened by cover, before the hunter could finish processing the hint of departing shadow.

Kneeling in the scrub, he placed his shotgun on the ground and took a deep drink of water. He shook his head, studying the path down which the gobbler had departed. Then he stood and laughed into the timber, mainly at himself for so amateurishly blundering into the turkey. Again, he reflected on what he had known for most of the years he had hunted.

Turkeys require thought.

— Joe Arnette, a free-lance writer from Maine, has written the "Last Call" column in Turkey & Turkey Hunting *since its first issue.*

CHAPTER 3

Satisfaction Defined: It's All in the Gobble

For hunters who have matured through years of pursuing turkeys, the gobble — not the kill — is the hunt's true experience.

■ JOHN J. WOODS

The wild turkey's gobble is among the unique sounds of the North American landscape. Avid turkey hunters would quickly rank the gobble No. 1, even when compared to the bugle of a bull elk or the honk of a Canada goose. Gobbling is an awesome, penetrating sound that arouses our hunting instincts.

For hunters who have matured through years of pursuing turkeys, the gobble — not the kill — is the hunt's true experience. With that in mind, here are some stories in which the gobble became the pinnacle of the hunt.

The Red Clover Gobbler

Preston Pittman's honeyhole for turkeys in southern Mississippi has been dubbed the Indian Mound Field. Pittman recalled a hunt when the field was covered with red-top clover, and a gobbler was turned on big time as dawn broke. The tom gobbled so vigorously and put on such a vibrant display of strutting, drumming and gobbling that Pittman was mesmerized.

"I can still close my eyes and see the bronze colors bouncing off that turkey in the red clover," Pittman said. "He was rotating into the sun in a full-fan strut. His gobbling was nonstop."

The gobbler continued his act for untold minutes, until he finally strolled within 16 yards of Pittman's gun. The tom strutted by and continued his display until he was 60 yards past. Not until the gobbler was out of range did Pittman realize he had never taken the safety off his shotgun.

"It dawned on me that I was supposed to shoot this bird," Pittman said. "I guess I was in a trance. The bird's gobbling sidetracked me, but it was worth it."

The Sunshine Gobbler

Ronnie Foy of Canton, Miss., is a self-taught turkey hunter with years of hunting and guiding experience. The Sunshine Gobbler was one of the most dazzling turkeys he can recall.

"His gobbling was always the same and revolved around sunlight patterns in the woods," Foy said.

No matter how Foy set up, the bird produced a pattern of teeth-rattling gobbles. His gobbling behavior — not the shot — became the hunt.

"I tried different things every morning I hunted this gobbler," Foy said. "I was looking for a common denominator, and I finally found one. That tom would only gobble when he was engulfed in a sunny spot in the woods. As he moved into the shadows, he went silent, and he stayed silent until he found another sunny spot to gobble and strut. He did that over and over."

On the surface, such behavior doesn't sound rare, because a tom will often display in sunlight. However, it's unusual to find a gobbler that only gets excited at the presence of sunshine in the woods.

Foy managed to take advantage of the pattern and lured the gobbler into a final strut in the sunshine.

"That gobbler was turned on to Vitamin D!" Foy said.

Two-Timing Gobblers

Dave Berkley, a decoy manufacturer, received the runaround from several hyperactive gobblers while testing his creations.

As Berkley was hunting turkeys in Arkansas on the Felsenthal National Wildlife Refuge a few years ago, a bevy of birds worked him into a fever.

"We set up against a backdrop of four gobbling turkeys, knowing we should score on one of them," he said. "Our decoys were out in front of a natural leaf screen, and one gobbler seemed especially excited by our calls."

That was just the start.

"If that bird gobbled once, he gobbled over 200 times in the next 30 minutes," Berkley said. "My pulse rate matched his gobbling. He went silent almost at the instant a second bird cranked it up to our right. Then, we could hear this gobbler running to us in the leaves. This new gobbler hung up at 40 yards, and then No. 1 tuned up again from the left. We were going absolutely nuts, thinking two birds were on us at the same time.

"The gobbling was so intense from these two birds that I was worn out. Suddenly, both gobblers walked away as I caught a glimpse of movement through the leafy underbrush. I leaned forward to separate the branches of our blind, and my jaw dropped to the ground. Both gobblers were walking away side by side. They were like old friends ready to share the seven hens strolling ahead of them."

The Machine Gun Gobbler

George Mayfield is an accomplished guide from Alabama's Black Warrior region. His guide service covers several states.

While hunting in Missouri a couple of years ago, Mayfield searched on foot for a new hunting area. The terrain consisted of tall, rolling hills and deep ravines.

"Around 9 a.m., I could barely make out what sounded like a tractor or pump running in the distance. It had a

Brian Lovett

rhythm that sounded funny to me, so I went to investigate.

"I worked my way around a hillside to a big narrow valley with a tall hill at the far end. The pumping sound was cranking away from the hilltop. It repeated every couple of seconds, 'cow-cow-cow,' in a constant rhythm. I crept forward until my senses were dumfounded. It was a turkey, and he was 'machine-gun gobbling.' I have no idea how that tom managed to do that over and over without stopping for a breath."

By that time, Mayfield was dying to see the tom, so he circled the hill through a thicket. Soon, he spotted the gobbler in full strut at 60 yards.

"I coaxed the gobbler into gun range and shut down his 'pump' forever," he said. "He was a 4-year-old longbeard that weighed 24 pounds. He was one gobbling-crazed bird I'll never forget."

The Legend of Ol' Club Foot

Doug Grann, the executive director of Wildlife Forever, has hunted turkeys for years and has a passion for gobbling birds. Ol' Club Foot, the legendary gobbler of Hoggie Ridge in Caledonia, Minn., made a lifelong impression on Grann.

Ol' Club Foot wasn't hindered by his handicap. In addition, he had a reputation as a gobbling fool and an uncanny sense of staying clear of a hunter's shotgun blast.

When Grann finally got to hunt the bird, the limping gobbler had fooled the landowner the previous day. However, the bird had disclosed his favorite roost tree. Sure enough, at daylight Ol' Clubfoot was home.

"Before leaving his roost, Ol' Club Foot gobbled at least 100 times, more than enough to get the adrenaline pumping," Grann said. "After teaming with another hunter, we split the ridge, with me on the southern end. After setting up, I used a slate to make some soft calls. Bam! Gobbles, double-gobbles and triple gobbles thundered across the ridge.

"My hunting partner's box calls fell on deaf ears, but every time I clucked or purred, Ol' Club Foot hit back with a resounding double gobble. At full light, the gobbler was still bellowing on his own, and I lost count at 123. After a while, the woods went silent."

At that point, Grann knew he was in the wrong place. He eased to the edge of a wheat field, and as he was about to step out, he looked up to see a gobbler sailing across Hoggie Ridge like a B-52 bomber. Ol' Club Foot hit the ground with a double gobble and went into full strut.

"My heart pounded at every gobble, but my yelps were drawing the gobbler closer," Grann said. "Those final four steps took forever, but my trigger finger tensed and the legend came to an end. The gobbler weighed 25 pounds, and he was missing one toe on his left foot. His gobbling show earned him a mount over my desk."

The Penny Arcade Gobbler

If you know how duck targets move at a carnival shooting gallery, you know how this tom worked. Two seasons ago, I set up on the edge of a field and began working a turkey at first light. From 6 a.m. to 11 a.m., the bird gobbled every five minutes.

His gobbling intrigued me. All morning, he seemed to move back and forth, right to left and then back again, like an arcade duck. It seemed as if the gobbler were on a railroad track. He never deviated from this mode, and he never stopped gobbling with intensity. He held his ground five hours, and though he always answered my calls, he never seemed secure in imitating an arcade duck.

Conclusion

Folks who appreciate a gobble more than the kill are usually seasoned hunters. Their attitude expresses respect for America's greatest game bird.

Hunters in this camp realize it's not always how many points you score, but how you score them. With turkey hunting, enjoying the gobble enhances the experience.

— John Woods is a longtime free-lance writer from Mississippi.

CHAPTER 4

Strange but True Turkey Hunts

Not all turkey hunts follow the rules. Consider these tales from the turkey twilight zone.

■ MICHAEL HANBACK

I clucked, and the turkey gobbled. I yelped, and the bird roared back. I cutt, and he cut loose with three gobbles! That old Virginia tom was a big talker but a slow walker. After hearing him gobble 50 times from the same spot, I decided to move.

I dropped off a ridge, circled and slipped in tight on the opposite side of the bird. I clucked, and he roared. I yelped, and he double-gobbled. You know the rest.

An hour later, the turkey begrudgingly drifted into sight. He wasn't a classic strutter, and he didn't work in like many gobblers, with his periscope up and his black eyes burning holes in the foliage. This tom duck-walked in with his crimson neck extended and low. He pecked the surrounding brush and the ground, gobbling the entire time.

I clucked on a diaphragm. The turkey roared but refused to lift his head. I yelped harder. He gobbled again, but still didn't expose his brain stem for me to shoot. All I could do was aim low, where the turkey's head was buried in some leaves. I pulled the shotgun's trigger, duff and dirt exploded, and the dead tom flopped down the ridge.

Back at camp, I cleaned the bird and found his crop stuffed with 1-inch-long cicadas. That sack was about to burst. I stopped counting at 60 of the slimy, green, big-eyed, thin-winged insects. The way I figure, the turkey probably pecked locusts between gobbling at my calls. How he double- and triple-gobbled while swallowing those bugs remains a mystery. However, it shows biologists aren't always right when they say breeding toms live almost entirely off their breast sponges during spring. I know one old longbeard that ate like a hog and talked with his mouth full.

Old Long Gobble

Legendary turkey hunter Ray Eye has a knack for encountering strange birds.

"One time, a hunter and I were walking and calling in the Ozarks of southern Missouri, hoping to strike a turkey," Eye said. "We heard a gobble down in a hollow, or at least we thought it was a gobble. It started out right — 'obbbblllleee' — but then it just kept going for 15 seconds or so. I listened to it three times. It wasn't a double or triple gobble — just one long, continuous stream of racket. I didn't know what the heck it was. I even thought some guy might be messing with me on a rubber gobble call."

With his curiosity piqued, Eye sneaked to a nearby field, set up and called. A huge tom with a long, thick beard strutted into the opening, extended his neck and wobbled a 12-second "obbbblllbbb-blllbbbbblllleeeeee." The turkey strutted in, long-gobbling the entire time.

"I guess the hunter came unglued, because he shot and missed clean as a whistle," Eye said.

Eye returned to the area a week later with another hunter. At daybreak an "obbbblllbbbbblllbbbbblllleeeeee" floated from a nearby ridge.

"What in the world was that?" the hunter asked.

"Oh, that's just old Long Gobble," Eye said. "Let's go get him."

Eye called, and the tom worked in. At 40 yards, the bird stuck out his neck and wobbled another booming 15-second gobble. This time, Eye got tickled, sat back in the leaves and tried to muffle his laughter. Somehow, the hunter kept his composure and killed the turkey.

"I walked up and checked Long Gobble's head," Eye said. "It was huge — as big and white as a softball — but it looked just like any old turkey head. I guess I should have dissected the head and neck right there to see where in the heck those gobbles came from. They sure were the weirdest turkey sounds I've heard."

Kamikaze and the Bullies

One spring, Eye headed to Massachusetts to hunt Yankee gobblers.

"That's where I ran into another bizarre bird," he said. "He'd often roost in a dead snag along an old road. You could

call to the turkey when it was pitch-black in the morning, and he'd fly down and run in. Three times, he strutted by gobbling, shuffling leaves and breaking sticks with his feet, but it was too dark to see him, much less shoot. Most turkeys don't feel comfortable walking around in the dark, but that bird sure did. He was so hot for a hen I named him The Kamikaze.

"And guess what? We never killed him. Every time I called to that turkey in daylight, he turned and went the other way."

A couple of years ago in Texas, world-class caller Walter Parrott shot a gobbler during the filming of a camouflage company video. The cameraman carried the big Rio to a

Brian Lovett

stock tank and washed the blood off its head and neck. He put the bird on the ground and spread its wings so it would look pretty for pictures later. The hunters then returned to their set-up trees.

"I want to get a few more shots of you calling," the videographer said. His camera whirred as Parrott floated a series of seductive clucks and yelps. Two more gobblers roared. The hunters watched incredulously as the longbeards ducked under a fence and strutted toward Parrott's dead turkey.

It's not unusual for a gobbler to jump atop a fallen tom and fight it with his spurs. But these birds were different.

"They hopped up on the gobbler and actually began treading on it," Parrott said with a laugh. "I kept calling, and

the birds kept treading. Pretty soon, they got bored and left. My turkey wasn't so pretty for pictures anymore."

Sunday's Gobbler

Call-maker Harold Knight had just returned to his Kentucky home after two weeks of hard hunting in Florida and Alabama. Just across the state line in Tennessee, spring turkey season opened the next day.

"I was a little apprehensive about going hunting again," he said. "I'd already been away from home a lot, and besides, the next day was Sunday morning. But hey, it was turkey season, so I went anyway."

Knight drove an hour in the pre-dawn gloom. When he got out of his truck and clicked the door shut, a turkey gobbled. He walked 200 yards, set up and called. The tom roared, flew down and began working in.

Knight looked into the silver morning sky and said, "Sir, you're really shining on me this morning." The gobbler's crinkled white head popped up in the foliage. Knight smiled, covered the bird and pulled the trigger.

Nothing happened. There was no boom, no click — nothing.

"I kept pulling and pulling the trigger, but the gun wouldn't fire," he said. "I got nervous, and pretty soon the gobbler did too. Finally, he turned and left."

Knight calmed his nerves and checked his shotgun. Sand and grit from his previous Southern hunts had accumulated in the gun's action and locked it tight.

"I laughed all the way back to the truck," Knight said. "I've seen just about everything imaginable in 43 years of turkey hunting, but it's not many mornings your gun doesn't fire. I guess it was just Sunday and not that turkey's time to meet the Creator."

That Pesky Pencil Beard

Most hunters assume the baddest gobbler in the springwoods is a bull of a bird — a 20-something pounder with a thick beard and spurs like stiletto blades. Dominant 3- and 4-year-old toms typically have grand looks, but many are 17-pound lightweights with frazzled beards. Consider Pencil Beard.

"That was the toughest Louisiana turkey I've ever hunted," said longtime turkey hunter and videographer Ron Jolly. "And he was a sight: skinny-bodied with 12 scraggly hairs on his chest that looked to be about 11 inches long."

Jolly hunted Pencil Beard every morning one spring.

"Most days, he traveled with 25 hens," he said. "No wonder that bird was so lean and mean."

On the season's final morning, Jolly slipped within spitting distance of Pencil Beard, who was roosted next to a huge briar patch.

"I've got you now," Jolly whispered to the bird. "There's no way you'll fly out into those briars. You'll have to pitch down on this hardwood ridge with me."

The turkey gobbled 100 times in the tree, hammering Jolly's soft calling.

"When day broke, he flew out in the middle of the briar patch, gobbled once and left," Jolly said. "That was the last

I ever heard and saw of old Pencil Beard. I'm sure he died of old age."

A Cowboy's Tale

I'd heard cattle and turkeys don't mix, but I never thought much about it. After all, I'd called in lots of birds strutting in green fields and meadows alongside beef and dairy stock. However, I endured a weird hunt in Texas a couple of years ago.

One April afternoon, I set up in a rancher's pasture and stroked sweet clucks and yelps on a slate call. I had a big turkey playing my game. The long-bearded Rio shimmered like a copper medicine ball in the brilliant sunshine. He strutted within 40 yards, and just as I prepared to pull the trigger, I caught movement out of the corner of my eye.

A cow clumped past my setup, mooed like crazy, and chased the gobbler out of the pasture back into a grove of oaks. After the shock of what I had witnessed wore off, I yanked down my facemask and whispered a string of unprintables. I figured the hunt was blown, and that I'd have to find another bird. But before I left, just for the heck of it, I cutt on a box call. The gobbler roared. I looked up and saw him coming again.

That cow spotted him, too. I watched helplessly as the big chunk of beef mooed and chased off the tom a second time.

I sat fuming for about 30 minutes, waiting for the cow to graze to the opposite end of the pasture. When he did, I cutt on a box call again. Amazingly, the gobbler bellowed and strutted in a third time. I shot him quickly, before the bovine could run over and mess things up.

Conclusion

For kicks on the hike out, I veered to where the cow was munching grass at the far end of the field. I know now what they say about cattle hating turkeys is true. I swear that animal looked at the longbeard over my shoulder and gave me a wicked smile.

— Michael Hanback, who writes Turkey & Turkey Hunting's *"Strategy Session" column, is one of the country's best-known turkey and big-game writers. He lives in Virginia.*

Brian Lovett

CHAPTER 5

The Issue of Ethics

What are ethics, anyway? And, just as important, how should we apply them to this activity we love so much?

■ JIM SPENCER

OK, turkey hunters, it's time for a three-part self-examination quiz. Part A is simple: All of you who consider yourselves ethical, law-abiding turkey hunters, raise your hands.

Hmm. Not bad. I see most of your hands in the air. Mine is raised, too.

Now for Part B. We don't need a show of hands this time, but think about each question and answer it — truthfully — to yourself.

The Honest Assessment

✔ Have you ever shot at a turkey that was maybe slightly out of range, hoping you might get lucky and kill it?

✔ Have you ever left litter on public or private property during or after a turkey hunt because you didn't want to be bothered carrying it until you got home?

✔ Have you ever hunted in a state with a half-day closure but stretched your hunt a few minutes past closing time because you were working a gobbler and he wouldn't come fast enough?

✔ Have you ever known a friend to violate a game law — take more than the legal limit of gobblers, for example, or start the season a day or two early — and said nothing because it's not nice to snitch on a buddy?

Brian Lovett

✔ Have you ever followed a gobbling turkey onto posted property without asking the landowner's permission?

✔ Have you ever hunted turkeys without a license, or the required tags or stamps, because you arrived for a hunt late the previous night, all the license dealers were closed, you didn't want to miss gobbling the next morning, and you told yourself you'd buy a license later?

✔ Have you ever used another person's tag on a turkey or let someone use yours?

✔ Have you ever shot a turkey still on the roost?

✔ Have you ever breasted out a turkey and thrown away the thighs and drumsticks because you didn't feel like bothering with them?

✔ Have you ever mistakenly shot a hen and left her in the field?

✔ Have you ever failed to tag or check a turkey, or looked the other way when one of your buddies did?

✔ Have you ever set up on a turkey and tried to call it away from another hunter who'd beaten you to the bird?

Now for Part C of our quiz. It's interchangeable with Part A, but I bet your answers won't be the same.

How many of you consider yourselves ethical, law-abiding turkey hunters?

In the Definition

Ethics. Sportsmanship. Turkey hunters hear those terms all the time, and we utter them with impunity.

But what are those things, anyway? And, just as important, how should we apply them to this activity we love so much?

If you're looking for concrete, hard-fact, cast-in-stone answers, you won't find them here. Better writers have tried to map out what constitutes ethical, sportsmanlike turkey

Brian Lovett

hunting behavior, and they've come up short every time. I have no delusions I'll do better.

If you don't think about it too deeply, you might be comfortable with the notion that turkey hunting regulations are acceptable parameters for what's ethical and what's not. After all, that's the job of state and federal wildlife managers — to tell us what we can and can't do while hunting or fishing. Therefore, they should have a handle on ethics, right?

I don't buy it.

For example, it's legal in my home state of Arkansas to sneak underneath a gobbler on the roost and blast him off his limb, provided you do it during the season and shooting hours (30 minutes before sunrise to sunset). Here in Razorback country, you could kill your annual limit that way year after year, brag about it on street corners and never get in trouble with wildlife officers. But don't tell me that's ethical.

In Missouri, you can't legally limb-swat a turkey. It's illegal. Further, Missouri doesn't allow afternoon hunting. It closes at 1 p.m.

Although Missouri and Arkansas have different turkey hunting regulations, the result of a hunt is still a dead gobbler, whether he was delimbed a half-hour before sunrise in Arkansas or called at 1:10 p.m. in Missouri. But in my opinion, one bird was killed unethically, and the other was not.

If a Missouri hunter called in and killed a bird 10 minutes past closing time, the act would be illegal but not unethical — except, of course, in the sense that it's unethical to break game laws.

However, is it always unethical to break game laws? If you answer that question quickly without thinking, your answer would certainly be "yes." But just as some legal acts are unethical, the reverse is also true. To illustrate, let me tell you a true story.

Tough Choices

Years ago, after I had just started turkey hunting, I went on a hunt with a friend. Tommy went one way along a big ridge in the Ouachita Mountains, and I went the other. About 8 a.m., we heard a shot, and each of us thought the other had killed a bird. But when we met at our prearranged rendezvous point later that morning, I noticed an odd look on Tommy's face. He questioned me about my hunt, asking where I'd gone, whether I had seen anything and if I had shot. He asked me the final question several times and finally asked me to come with him. Down the ridge in the direction he'd hunted, he went to a ravine and raked back a pile of leaves to reveal a freshly killed hen.

"I found her laying on the top of the ridge right about where we split up to hunt," Tommy said. "Are you sure you didn't shoot this morning?"

I hadn't and assured him again. After debating the pros and cons of the situation, we made an uncomfortable decision. I hope the coons and bobcats enjoyed their windfall that night.

Neither Tommy nor I were brave enough to do what we wanted, which was to bring that hen off the mountain and eat her for supper. That was — and is — our ethic: to not waste game. And as surely as day follows night, we deliberately wasted that turkey. But in our defense, if we had been caught with the bird, we'd have been ticketed. Telling a game warden the truth would have sounded ridiculous, and we knew it.

So the coons ate well that night, while Tommy and I had bologna sandwiches. We were pristinely legal, but we felt like dirt.

Tommy and I still fret about that long-ago decision. We acted within the law. Any other action would have put us outside it. But did we act ethically? We think not, but we're still not sure.

Obvious and Subtle

Outdoor ethics. You find the subject cropping up in the most unlikely places. Listen to Pat Conroy, author of notable works such as *The Great Santini* and *The Lords of Discipline*, in the prologue of *The Prince of Tides*. Tom Wingo, the guy played by Nick Nolte in the movie, is talking:

"When I was 10, I killed a bald eagle for pleasure, for the singularity of the act, despite the divine, exhilarating beauty of its solitary flight over schools of whiting. It was the only thing I had ever killed that I had never seen before. After my father beat me for breaking the law and for killing the last eagle in Colleton County, he made me build a fire, dress the bird, and eat its flesh as tears rolled down my face. Then he turned me over to Sheriff

Benson, who locked me in a cell for over an hour. My father took the feathers and made a crude Indian headdress for me to wear to school. He believed in the expiation of sin. I wore the headdress for weeks, until it began to disintegrate feather by feather. Those feathers trailed me in the hallways of the school as though I were a molting, discredited angel."

"Never kill anything that's rare," my father had said.

"I'm lucky I didn't kill an elephant," I replied.

"You'd have had a mighty square meal if you had," he answered.

This idea of, "Don't kill it if you don't intend to eat it" is a recurrent theme in outdoor ethics. However, proper ethical behavior for a turkey hunter goes farther and deeper.

Someone once said ethics are what you do when no one is looking. And there, in a nutshell, is the potential pitfall: Almost everything a turkey hunter does occurs when no one is looking. We have abundant opportunity to engage in sneaky behavior. Like football, turkey hunting has rules of ethics and sportsmanship. But unlike football, there are usually no referees on the field.

That's why ethics are so important for the turkey hunter. There's no one in stripes standing around with flag and whistle to make us play by the rules. If you grab a defensive tackle's facemask during a football game, somebody will blow a whistle and step off yardage against your team. If you set up on a gobbler another hunter is working, there's no penalty, even if someone sees you. It's another example of an unethical act that's not illegal.

The Personal Mindset

Ethics, when you knock the bark off them, are expressions of morality. And because your morals are personal, morality can't be effectively legislated. Neither can ethics. Most state wildlife agencies give ethics lots of coverage in hunter education courses, but I believe it's mostly a waste of time. By the time children appear in a hunter ed class at age 12 or 13, their mind set is already established. They're on their way to becoming ethical hunters — in which case, you're preaching to the choir — or they're headed the other way, in which case, you're preaching to the deaf.

But we still have to wrestle with it. Turkey hunting, by its secluded and reclusive nature, is vulnerable to ethics violations. And as the sport continues to become more popular and the woods become crowded, it's inevitable conflicts between hunters will increase. How we handle those will affect our enjoyment of turkey hunting and our right to continue it.

Wingo, munching on the stringy flesh of his eagle, no doubt formed some definite ideas regarding acceptable and unacceptable outdoor behavior. Tommy and I, chewing bologna sandwiches and thinking about the dead hen we left in the woods, didn't form any. If an eagle flew in front of Wingo, smart money says he wouldn't pull the trigger. Whether Tommy or I would bring the hen in next time is still in question.

The basic issue with which we must wrestle isn't just, "Is it legal?" but also, "Is it right?"

The Golden Rule is a good yardstick, but it's not the only one.

Conclusion

There are no black-and-white answers. The issue of turkey hunting ethics is as full of thorns as a multiflora rose thicket. But because you asked, I'll give you my parameters for establishing what constitutes unethical turkey hunting behavior and what doesn't. I ask myself three questions:

✔ If everybody did it, would it damage the sport or turkey populations?

✔ If I do this, will it bother anyone?

✔ Would I still do this if someone could see me?

If the answer to any of those is "yes," it's unethical.

— Jim Spencer, contributing editor for Turkey & Turkey Hunting, *is a confirmed turkey hunting addict from Arkansas.*

Brian Lovett

CHAPTER 6

Reflections on Putting

It might be the most dreaded sound in the spring woods, but it sure gets your attention.

■ *LAURIE LEE DOVEY*

As Mac Drake and I positioned ourselves along a gentle hillside next to a massive field, I had little faith. We'd spent 10 hours zigzagging the hardwoods of west-central Georgia unsuccessfully searching for a March gobbler. If Drake and I hadn't known the area was thick with toms, we might not have returned. Our time afield had been arduous.

The Blink of an Eye

I was fatigued and welcomed Drake's suggestion to finish the day calling a little, perhaps getting lucky but mostly listening for birds traveling toward roosts. It was only my sixth or seventh turkey hunt, so summoning the patience to sit quietly the rest of the day was impossible.

After 20 or 30 minutes of sitting, intensely studying the terrain and listening to Drake call occasionally from the hillside above me, I turned to him, shrugged my shoulders and pulled down my headnet.

"I've had enough," I said. "How about helping me with my calling?"

"Sure," Drake said.

I set my shotgun on the ground, stripped off my gloves, headnet, hat and cumbersome turkey vest, and skipped 15 yards up the hill to sit by Drake. As the sun sank toward the horizon, Drake showed me how to yelp, cluck, putt, purr and cutt on box and slate calls. He'd call two or three times, and then I'd try. Often, we'd laugh at my efforts — shrill screeches, rasping grates or peg movements that created no sound. That time was among my most memorable in turkey hunting. It was what hunting was about — veterans sharing their love, enthusiasm and knowledge with novices who glowed from anticipation and excitement.

Hello There

Glancing at my watch, I realized we'd been calling, laughing and talking for an hour. We were scheduled to meet some hunting companions soon, so I suggested we gather our gear and ease to the rendezvous location while listening for birds.

I had to walk down the hill to get my gun and vest. Standing, I turned to scan the knoll above and behind us and stretch muscles that had suffered a long day of abuse. When I turned, I stared at a gobbler 20 yards away.

I'm not sure if the tom or I was more surprised or confused about how to react. I gasped, and the turkey putted so loudly I almost fell backward down the hill. Instead, I froze and was stared down by a 20-plus-pound tom.

"Putt, putt, putt!"

The bird continued but didn't move. I mimicked it, feeling like a gunslinger in a gunfight — waiting and wondering who would draw first. However, I didn't have my gun. It was out of reach a few yards behind me.

Without thinking, I dropped to my knees behind the lip of the knoll.

"Turkey!" I said to Drake.

"Get your gun," he said.

"Putt, putt, putt!"

We heard furious wingbeats, and then laughed uncontrollably.

Who said you have to be a great caller to attract a gobbler?

A Different Twist

I don't enjoy the pressure of having my turkey hunts videotaped. I've done some stupid things, including falling flat on my face, missing a gobbler at 20 steps, tearing my trousers on a barbwire fence, and falling asleep at my setup only to wake up and see a gobbler feeding 30 yards away. Having these incidents filmed is embarrassing, and it provides longtime ammunition for jokes. Occasionally, though, I've let friends film me.

That was the case last spring during a Missouri hunt with Lohman. Randy Marcum, a cameraman, and Ricky Joe Bishop, a multiple Grand National calling champion, guided me.

We were hunting farmland where birds concentrated in small woodlots that interrupted open terrain. During the second morning of our hunt, we slipped across a pasture before first light. We had to travel across huge fields, and our movement would have been spotted by birds 300 to 400 yards away. We were careful not to make a sound as we crossed from the field to the woods near a roosting area.

Gang War

Darkness still controlled the morning as we selected trees that would provide cover. As we settled in, I remembered the previous morning, when we'd worked several birds that never traveled into range. Later that day, we worked three toms to within 35 yards of my gun. I had missed one cleanly — on tape. I was embarrassed. I prayed for redemption, not a replay, knowing the videotape would be rolling.

Bishop and I were still fussing with our vests, calls and gloves when a gobble plastered us to our set-up tree. A gobbler was roosted less than 30 yards from us. Within 10 minutes, several other toms and hens sounded off within 50 yards. Bishop and I were concerned. Even if the birds didn't see us when light filtered into the area, we wouldn't be able to call or move.

We discussed getting out of Dodge. However, we couldn't talk to Marcum, who was too far away. He motioned to us, but Bishop and I didn't understand if he was telling us to abandon the site or sit tight. We decided to stay put.

Within minutes, the treetops exploded with sound. Dozens of birds — maybe 40 or more — started calling. A mix of toms, jakes and hens had apparently surrounded the field the night before, and now they'd lost control. They yelped, cutt, gobbled and clucked at each other. It was exciting and nerve-racking. Waves of goose bumps undulated across my skin. I'd never heard anything like it.

A Target Emerges

I couldn't breathe, and I wondered how I should handle the situation. My predominant thought was that, as the light increased, if we moved, the exodus of turkeys would resemble a riot. We could identify the incongruous outlines of five or six birds in the bare tree branches in front of us.

My focus was diverted when another bird roosted on the opposite side of the field pitched into the middle of the field. Because it was still dark, I was confident I could ease 90 degrees to my left so I could watch the bird. I moved slowly and deliberately. Bishop remained still to watch the roosted birds. We were sitting back to back with the tree between us. Marcum and his camera were pointed at the field and the bird on the ground.

I strained my eyes through the darkness and fog but couldn't discern whether the turkey was a hen or a gobbler. Seconds later, a thunderous gobble and an outstretched neck betrayed the bird. I nestled low against the tree and focused on the tom. I tried to ignore the boisterous choir of birds around us, which my tom seemed to be conducting. His melody of gobbles was backed by thunderous refrains from each section of the choir.

During the next 30 minutes — it might have been 20 or 45 minutes, I'm not sure — my tom strutted, pranced, spun and gobbled. As each minute passed, he stepped closer to the decoy 20 yards from me and in line with my gun. I played dozens of scenarios in my head. I knew we were minutes from having 15 to 20 birds in the field, which would prohibit a shot or movement. I prayed for the bird to come closer, begging it to close the gap so I could shoot before the rowdy crowd moved into the field.

Try to Ignore Him

I was so focused that I barely acknowledged the wingbeats behind me. However, I immediately recognized panic in Bishop's voice as he said, "Don't move, don't move." I froze just as I was ready to make my final gun and head adjustments.

Time stopped. Suddenly, I was almost lifted off the ground by a piercing putt from behind me. My shoulders fell from disappointment. I thought the hunt was finished and was sure we'd been busted. However, only two gobblers on the ground behind me moved, and my tom didn't seem concerned about the other gobbler's putting.

A tom behind me putted again, louder and more shocking than the first time. I cringed, but my tom didn't. The third putt sounded like Bishop calling. That's how close

the bird was to us. There was so much action, I couldn't keep track of everything.

A hen flew into the field from my left. Strutting, my tom took several steps toward me but veered left toward the hen. The putting tom was walking somewhere behind me, and the gang of roosted birds continued shaking the treetops. Another tom set its wings and pitched into the field as if on a bombing mission. It had targeted my tom. When the diving gobbler spooked my bird, I was distracted by the barrage of gobbling, cackling, clucking, yelping and putting. Finally, I decided the noise and the birds surrounding me didn't matter.

A Positive Conclusion

I identified two openings through the branches of the hemlock umbrella that hid me from the birds in the field. I decided I'd shoot through either of the openings if my tom stepped into a window of opportunity. I also decided to follow my tom with my shotgun barrel, no matter what the consequences. As a result, I was unaware of anything but my tom and the turkeys near him. I heard nothing.

When the gobbler stepped into the first opening, a hen was too close to him. I couldn't shoot. I only had one chance left, and I had to make a big move to get into position. My tom moved into the second opening, and the hen moved out of the way. My shotgun sounded, and the gobbler fell.

For the next 30 minutes, I could barely talk, walk or breathe. I shook as if stricken by seizures. But we got the hunt on film, and my moment of redemption was sweet.

For once, putting hadn't indicated failure.

— Laurie Lee Dovey is a free-lance writer from Georgia.

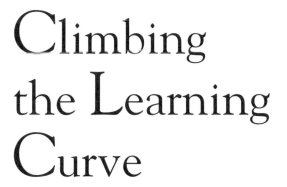

CHAPTER 7

Climbing the Learning Curve

Becoming a good turkey hunter isn't a destination — it's a direction. The author has endured trials and tribulations during his climb up the learning curve, but his experiences can help you along the same path.

■ JIM SPENCER

The first gobbler I killed was called in for me by another hunter. I had tried for four springs to do it on my own, ever since my first hunt.

During that unforgettable first hunt, I heard seven Mississippi gobblers sound off in row-row-row-your-boat style, in response to a barred owl hoot. I became an instant turkey hunting junkie.

But not a good one, you understand. I wasn't even a mediocre one. The guy who took me turkey hunting that morning didn't know much more about it than I did, so we didn't kill a bird. Looking back with the accumulated experience of a quarter-century of chasing turkeys, it's easy to remember several occasions during that turkey-rich hunt when we should have killed gobblers.

Brian Lovett

Of course, we didn't capitalize because we were too far down the learning curve.

The Slow Climb

Following the tradition established on that inaugural hunt, I spent the next four Aprils chasing gobblers without killing any.

I blundered, bumbled and botched chance after chance. I made mistakes I didn't even know were mistakes. I did every stupid thing you could think of in the turkey woods, and then for good measure, I did them again.

After four springs of it, I got fed up. I tried one last time, got ring-around-the-rosied by two gobblers the same morning and swore off turkey hunting for good. Spring mornings were too good for bass fishing to waste any more of them hunting oversized birds that wouldn't cooperate, I explained to everyone who would listen.

"To heck with turkeys," I said.

A friend got wind of it and called me.

"You're not quitting yet," he said. "You're going turkey hunting with me next Saturday."

Despite my initial objections, that's what we did — and sure enough, we got skunked. We didn't even hear a gobble. During the drive home after a grueling, dawn-to-dusk hunt, I swore off turkey hunting again, but Robert talked me into giving it one more try the next Saturday.

Sometimes nowadays in April when things are going badly, I still wonder whether it was good that I killed a gobbler that morning. He wasn't much, that first gobbler: 18 pounds, an 8-inch pencil-beard and spurs that looked like miniature Hershey's Kisses — your typical late-hatched 2-year-old after a poor mast crop and a tough winter. But there he lay, shot in the head, and that counted for a lot.

As Robert and I stood on opposite sides of that gobbler, shaking hands across the bird's still-quivering body, Robert spoke two sentences I remember as clearly as everything else that fine spring morning.

"OK, buddy," he said, "the ice is broken. Now you're on your own."

Knowledge is Power

When you knock all the feathers off it, that's what turkey hunting is about — being on your own. Sure, it's nice to go hunting with someone who knows a lot more about the sport than you do, because it gives you a fast track on picking up good stuff about turkey hunting. That's no doubt the best way to get started in this frustrating sport. However, your goal as a turkey hunter should be to get past the point of needing in-the-woods mentoring.

I've been lucky in my turkey hunting career. As a guy who writes magazine articles about the sport, I've hunted with some of the best in the business — people named Salter, Harris, Walker, Brown, Norton, Haas, Strickland, Drury, Pittman, Jordan, Waddell and Eye — those guys. And I've learned a lot from every one.

However, those famous folks aren't the only top-shelf turkey hunters out there. You'll find hundreds, maybe thousands, of turkey hunters who are every bit as good as those well-known hunters, but haven't been in position to receive the publicity to become famous outside their local area.

They're just regular men and women — local hunters who have achieved expert status. Chances are, you know some of these people. If you want a crash course in turkey hunting, somehow wrangle a hunting invitation with one of them.

Brian Lovett

The only trouble is those experts are often older hunters, people who learned to hunt gobblers in those dim, bleak days of the 1940s, '50s and '60s, when turkey populations hadn't started recovering. There weren't many turkeys then — and even fewer turkey hunters — and reliable information was almost nonexistent. Those guys learned to hunt turkeys in the school of hard knocks, and they learned to guard their intelligence with the care of wartime generals. Most of these old-guard hunters can't seem to break that habit. Many are loners, and some are downright unfriendly. Their attitude seems to be, "Hey, I learned this stuff on my own. I'll be damned if I'll show any of it to you."

Fortunately, the brightest bulb on the tree isn't the only one that sheds light. Plenty of lesser luminaries are pretty good turkey hunters, and although this group also has loners and information misers, you'll find many folks who'll take

time to help. You might not have much luck getting invitations to go turkey hunting with these folks, but it's not difficult to find somebody who'll let you pick his brain. The only thing a dedicated turkey hunter likes more than talking about hunting turkeys is hunting turkeys. Take advantage of that at seminars, calling contests, sport shows and National Wild Turkey Federation banquets.

Speaking of which, involvement in a state or local National Wild Turkey Federation chapter is one of the best ways for a neophyte hunter to upgrade his skill level. As a former 5-year banquet committee co-chairman and former NWTF Arkansas State Chapter board member, I know firsthand how much knowledge rubs off on when you spend time working with other turkey hunters.

It also helps to hunt with a partner when you're trying to climb the learning curve. My friend Bill and I formed a loose partnership when we were still pretty far down the curve, and we hunted together more often than not.

Paying the Bills

When Bill and I were trying to double-team a bird, we held whispered conversations to discuss almost every move of every hunt, thinking things through before we did them. Some conversations got pretty heated, and I'm sure some of them went on so long the gobblers got bored and went somewhere else. However, we taught each other a lot in the process, and we killed our share of turkeys.

When we didn't hunt together, Bill and I got together afterward and shared experiences through lengthy conversations and explanations that lasted almost as long as the hunts. We dissected each hunt, discussing the pros and cons of a strategy, and what we could have done differently to make things turn out better. When one of us got lucky and killed a gobbler, we dissected those hunts even more meticulously, striving to understand what we did — or didn't do — to kill the bird and why our strategy worked. That also made us better hunters.

There's a wealth of second-hand information nowadays that wasn't available even two decades ago, and that accumulated knowledge can also help you climb the curve. Turkey hunting seminars are included in almost every sporting convention and sports show, and these interactive seminars feature some of the best, most articulate hunters in the business. An hour at one of those seminars is worth a spring of "uh-oh, wish-I-hadn't-done-that" lessons in the woods.

And don't get me started on books and videos. My turkey hunting library contains more than 80 videos and 50 books, and I buy every new one I hear about. (I have three books on order as I write this.) And if I've thrown away an outdoor magazine with a turkey hunting article in it, it was an accident.

However, reading about turkey hunting and watching seminars and videos will only take you so far up the curve. Educational opportunities are extremely valuable, but there's no way they can replace experience. You must get out and take your lumps while trying to put that book knowledge into practice.

In the Woods

Pay attention to what's happening when you're in the woods. That sounds like the worst sort of useless advice, but I've watched beginner after beginner go through a turkey hunt like a steel ball in a pinball machine, bouncing from

Mark Drury

bumper to bumper and not learning a blessed thing in the process. Every action or nonaction has consequences in the turkey woods, and hunters who note these cause-and-effect relationships and think about how to deal with them climb the learning curve farther and faster.

Take your time when hunting. One of the biggest mistakes turkey hunters of all experience levels make is hurrying.

Remember, a turkey isn't on a timetable. He has all day to do whatever he wants — and if he doesn't get to it today, there's always tomorrow. Some hunting situations require quick decisions and fast action, but usually, speed is not only unnecessary but also detrimental. Be deliberate, and think things through.

One way to help this learning-curve business is to keep a hunting log. When you spook a turkey or screw up a hunt in one of the myriad ways possible, record it — honestly — in your log. Also, write why you think your mistake was a mistake, and speculate about what you might have done differently.

This will make you think. More importantly, it will create a permanent record of your experiences. I reread my turkey log every year during the off-season. It helps me get through the awful heebie-jeebies that I experience on long February evenings, and it reminds me of the things I've learned through my lengthy enrollment in the school of hard knocks.

Passing it On

Don't forget, as you begin to accumulate knowledge that helps you climb the curve, you don't have to be a terribly good hunter to help another fellow who's farther down the curve.

Case in point: I was at work one April morning almost 15 years ago when I received a call from a fellow who started talking in a rush almost before I had time to answer. He was a beginning turkey hunter, he said, and was having trouble getting things to go his way. He had read some of my stuff in magazines and figured that if he could only tag along with somebody who knew a little bit about hunting turkeys, he might get a toe-hold on this fascinating, frustrating sport. Please, please, please would I take him hunting, he asked.

He wouldn't even carry a gun; he just wanted to tag along and pick up a few pointers.

I wasn't very far up the curve at that time, and I told him so.

"That doesn't matter," he said. "No matter how much you think you don't know, you know more than me. I don't even know enough to know when I'm screwing up."

Well, I know déjà vu when I hear it. I remembered the helpless, hopeless feeling I carried through four years of my floundering, pitiful beginning as a turkey hunter, and I knew how that guy felt. It didn't hurt, either, when he told me his name — more déjà vu — was Robert. We made a date.

Lo and behold, the next Saturday morning, we struck a cooperative gobbler that answered my late-morning hoot. He came obligingly to my mediocre calling, and Robert killed him. And as we stood over that other first bird, which wasn't much of a bird either, I told Robert the student the two sentences I'd heard from Robert my mentor six or seven springs earlier:

"OK, buddy, the ice is broken," I said. "Now you're on your own."

It felt good to say it. It feels even better today, because Robert the student has become a pretty fair turkey hunter. He's even mentored other beginners, and it feels good to think about that, too.

On Course

It's fair to say I'm a better turkey hunter than when I called in Robert's first bird in the late 1980s. Certainly, I'm better than when the other Robert called my first one in for me. I've got a long way to go, but I've hunted those magnificent birds long enough to have learned the two most important things about turkey hunting:

First, never take anything for granted, because there will never be two turkey hunts that play out the same.

Second, there is no end to the learning curve, because becoming a good turkey hunter isn't a destination.

It's a direction.

— *Jim Spencer, contributing editor for* Turkey & Turkey Hunting, *is a confirmed turkey hunting addict from Arkansas.*

Brian Lovett

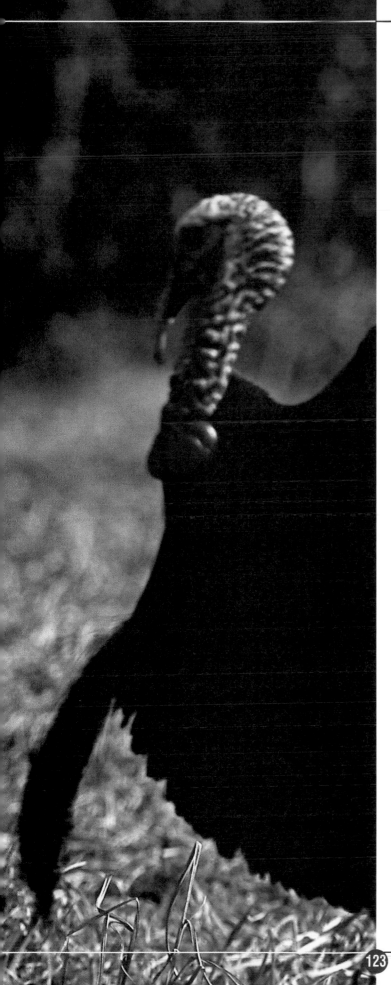

CHAPTER 8

What Can Go Wrong Now?

Turkey hunters inevitably talk about gobblers that seemed like dead ducks but turned around and kicked the hunter in the seat of the pants. These birds burn in the brains of veteran hunters.

■ SCOTT BESTUL

My wife, Shari, has a favorite pastime when friends visit during turkey season. When the conversation turns to turkeys, she asks our guests if they'd like to watch a video. Because turkey addicts flock to videos like gadgeteers to Global Positioning System units, our guests rush to our television. Then Shari pops in The Tape, a beautiful piece of cinematography in which I miss a gobbler with my bow. At 10 steps. Twice.

Filmed by my friend Ron Gehrke, The Tape has become a spring staple in the Bestul house; a celluloid reminder of a gobbler with a death wish as large as Wyoming and the hunter who couldn't kill him.

I've memorized the film; the hard-gobbling, brush-bearded tom, walking purposely up the hill toward our setup; the breathtaking strutting pauses; and Ron's masterful cluck, which stops the bird in my shooting lane. Then, there's the arrow passing harmlessly under the turkey's breast.

There's a brief pause as the longbeard runs off for a couple of minutes and gathers his wits in nearby cover. Then, there's an ear-splitting gobble, Gehrke and I scrambling to regroup and find a call, and the certain parade of the gobbler back to the same shooting lane.

The second arrow comes somewhat closer. That's verified by the footage, which shows my tracking string tangled in the tom's legs as he sprints downhill, finally tired of my incompetence.

I've taken plenty of kidding about that film, but it's among my most cherished memories. I've gotten lucky on a few birds since then, including a few that made the star of The Tape look small. But I'll never forget that turkey — the one that should have died but didn't, and that lived as an example of how wrong a hunt can go when everything seems right.

Fortunately, I'm not the sole possessor of hard luck. When I chat with guides and other experts, they inevitably talk about gobblers that seemed like dead ducks but turned around and kicked the hunter in the seat of the pants. These birds burn in the brains of veteran hunters.

Tad and the Bad Turkey

Usually, a predicable tom is a goner. A gobbler that roosts in one spot and conducts its daily routine in a tight core area is often destined to die. Tad Brown, call designer for M.A.D. Calls and a hunter known for killing tough turkeys, has pursued a predictable Missouri gobbler for years but has yet to to pull the trigger on him.

"I've been after this tom for 4 years now," Brown said. "He lives on one of my old haunts, and I can't figure him out. He's always on the same ridge. You can roost him in the same spot every night or find him in that area if you slip in the next morning. He has a hard, authoritative gobble I recognize every time.

"The trouble is, he'll only gobble once. It's always the first gobble of the morning, and then he's done. I've slipped in tight to him a couple of times and tried to work him, but he cools right down. He just shuts up, and you don't hear him anymore."

The gobbler varied his routine once — with surprising results.

"Me, Mark (Drury) and Jim Spencer were in on him last year, and he did his one gobble," Brown said. "But there was a trio of mature birds in the same area, and pretty soon they fired up and were coming in hard. So we switched to them, but just when we thought we'd see them, from behind us this first turkey gobbles one time, hard and loud. Well, those other three just shut down. And you know, I've never killed

Brian Lovett

Brian Lovett

a turkey in that spot since he's been there. It's like he has to prove he's a tough guy and mess with all the other gobblers. That's why I call him a bad turkey."

Despite the bird's toughness, Brown hasn't given up on him.

"Birds like that just get under your skin," he said. "He's a phantom. I think he's just one of those gobblers that hangs by himself and doesn't really want company. I believe strongly that turkeys, like people, have distinct personalities, and this one is just different. I think the only way to kill him is spend a couple of days with him, and that's tough when so many other birds will gobble good and come hard. I don't know if I can kill him, but I intend to try."

The Endurance Contest

As one of Wisconsin's top turkey guides, Gehrke has worked many tough longbeards. However, a gobbler he

hunted with his son Wayne last spring stands out. Gehrke and his son were on a military base loaded with birds. The base's extensive oak flats provide ideal turkey habitat, but they're mixed with small swamp holes.

"This bird seemed to hit almost every call I'd throw at him," Gehrke said. "Several times, he'd come close, but then he'd retreat across one of these little swamps to an island of oaks."

The walking got tough, but the pair stuck with the gobbler.

"We'd get on an island with him, let things settle down, and I'd call," Gehrke said. "He'd crawl all over it, gobbling aggressively. I'd tell Wayne to get the gun up, and then the bird would fade off and head into the swamp again. I kept listening for a hen with him, but I couldn't hear one, so I kept at him. I figured he'd break soon, because he was gobbling so hard."

The chase led into a swamp, and the gobbler reached an island with the hunters close behind.

"We'd set up and call, and he'd climb on it," Gehrke said. "I tried all the tricks — scratching in the leaves, breaking a little twig, switching calls — but nothing seemed to break him. He'd gobble for a while, no more than 40 or 50 yards out, and then head to another island. This went on for 2½ hours."

With closing time nearing, Gehrke and his son followed the bird to a final island.

"I had thrown every call in my vest at him except my gobble tube," he said. "So I decided we had nothing to lose. I gobbled at him. There was a long pause and no response. Then finally, we heard a hard gobble and then another. I gobbled at him again, and he hit that right away. Then I could hear a bird coming through the leaves, and I told Wayne to get his gun up. But the tom started gobbling again, and he wasn't the bird we heard walking. Finally, a lone hen popped out, coming to our gobbling, and the tom stayed in the background, gobbling in frustration that his hen would leave him.

"But he finally broke to follow her and popped into an opening 20 yards out. Wayne's shot took 3 inches off the side of a tree near the bird, and the gobbler flew out of there untouched. I just collapsed in a heap on the ground. I was completely wrung out."

The Mexican Hat Dance

Traveling to Mexico for Gould's turkeys seemed exciting to Pat Reeve, a top-notch hunter and then-videographer for Hunter's Specialties. Gould's hunting opportunities are becoming more available for Americans, and Reeve was part of a group that visited Sonora's Sierra Occidental Mountains in Spring 1998. You'd think lightly hunted wilderness birds would be pushovers. However, Reeve discovered that wasn't true.

"It started just plain scary," he said. "We had quite a long drive from the airport to the ranch, driving through mountain roads. We came around a bend, and there was a group of Mexican police or federales — we were never quite sure what — blocking the road. They were heavily armed, and they had guns pointing at us the whole time. It was a remote area, we knew no Spanish, and they went through everything we had. I don't know what they were looking for. Thank goodness we didn't have any guns, but we did have thousands of dollars of camera gear. It was the only time in my life I've felt I had no control over my life, and I was very scared."

After a long, tense standoff, the armed group let the hunters pass. The next morning, Reeve and the group's other veteran hunters quickly gained respect for Gould's.

"Those birds had me up in arms from the beginning," he said. "I had absolutely no clue why they'd do the things they'd do. Birds would gobble well off the roost, we'd set up on them, and they'd fly down and go the opposite way. Even when you had the terrain to your advantage, they'd go straight over the mountain away from you. It was like they went out of their way to avoid your calls."

Despite the region's abundant birds, the gringos had difficulty getting on a gobbler.

"We gained a lot of respect for our guides that trip," Reeve said. "They knew where birds would be, and frequently it was in some remote canyon 30 miles from the lodge. The terrain is so vast out there, knowing where to start was just a mystery."

Finally, after many unsuccessful setups, Reeve and partner Tom Miranda had a bird come to their calling.

"He was double- and triple-gobbling, strutting all the way," he said. "We thought finally we were going to get a kill on tape. As he got into gun range, we could see it was a jake. We couldn't believe it. We finally managed to kill a tom the last morning of the hunt, but it was almost by mistake. We just set up in a feeding area, managed to call a hen in, and the tom just followed her. It seems you call in the whole flock down there or nothing at all."

The Rebellious Rio

Gary Roberson of Burnham Brothers Game Calls has come face to face with many turkeys while guiding and hunting in Texas. But the toughest gobbler he's encountered left an impression.

"I was the host for Bruce Brady, his wife, Peggy, and Ronnie Strickland of Mossy Oak for a hunt on a ranch near the Llano River in Texas," Roberson said. "After two days of hunting, we encountered a Rio gobbler we nicknamed Terrible Tom. For three days, we watched him behave as aggressively as any gobbler I'd seen."

The Bradys first encountered the gobbler while calling to a trio of longbeards.

"The three toms were strutting just out of gun range but not gobbling," Roberson said. "Finally, one of the three sounded off, and another bird answered from 600 yards away. It was Terrible Tom, and he came to the trio at a dead run. When he reached them, he positioned himself in front of the birds and paced back and forth. When one of the birds dropped his wings, Tom flew up and crashed down on him, knocking him to the ground. He was on top of the other bird for several moments, and the Bradys thought Tom would kill the other gobbler.

"After Tom hopped off the fallen gobbler, he stared at the other birds and then walked slowly away. The beaten bird eventually got up and joined his comrades in a hasty retreat."

The hunters also saw Tom the next day.

"When the sun rose, there was only one bird gobbling and it was Terrible Tom," Roberson said. "Every other bird was amazingly quiet. Tom hit the calls that Bruce made and came running. But he hung up at about 80 yards and wouldn't come any farther. However, he gobbled more than 200 times that morning.

"That afternoon, we were hunting the same area when we struck another trio of gobblers that came to our calls. As they approached, another gobbler emerged from the cover and ran at them. It was Tom, and he chased the birds more than 300 yards. Then he turned to our calls. He gobbled his way back to our setup, stopping to strut on the way. He came as close as 60 yards but hung up when his instincts took over. He was the king and knew the hens should come to him."

Tom was at it again the third day.

"He gobbled well off the roost from a pecan tree 400 yards downriver," Roberson said. "He flew down immediately and ran toward us, stopping every 50 yards to gobble and strut. It seemed like an easy kill, with no hens around and him fresh off the roost. But at 80 yards, he slowed and began circling us. We threw every call we knew at him, but he wouldn't budge for a solid hour. We realized this was probably an unkillable bird."

However, fortune intervened.

"Another gobbler came in to about 100 yards and let out a gobble," Roberson said. "The bright red of Tom's head turned blue with anger, and he gobbled sharply at the advancing bird and then started toward him. In his attempt to cut off his opposition, Tom walked to within 40 yards, and I was able to make the shot.

"I wish I could say great calling ended his reign, but if it hadn't been for that other gobbler, Terrible Tom would be there today. The same dominance that made him such a trophy led to his demise."

— *Scott Bestul, a longtime contributing editor for* Turkey & Turkey Hunting, *hails from the turkey-rich hills of southeastern Minnesota.*

Brian Lovett

Brian Lovett

The Ambush

Ambushing a turkey is nothing new, but is there a right or wrong time to do so? Further, is ambushing a turkey ethical? Is it OK some, none or all of the time? Really, it's a personal choice.

■ JOHN TROUT JR.

Some hunters consider it unethical to ambush a gobbler. Others don't. Imagine calling for hours to an eager-sounding gobbler, only to have someone ambush the bird before it comes within range.

That's what I experienced opening morning two years ago in southwestern Indiana.

The Slip-In Slob

I heard a gobbler at dawn and quickly moved to an old strip-mined area featuring small, steep hills. I used the terrain to my advantage, staying out of sight and finally setting up just over a hilltop from the noisy bird.

I called softly, and the bird answered four times. A few minutes passed, and he gobbled again. I called again, and we communicated for the next 30 minutes. Then, however, I heard the soft yelps of a hen with the gobbler. Neither of the birds walked over the hill.

After the turkeys moved to my left, I followed. Again, we communicated, and again, the turkeys moved farther away. During the next hour, the gobbler answered every call and came into view — out of range — twice. He was probably the most cooperative turkey I've worked.

After three hours, it seemed perseverance would pay. The hen came into view atop a hill, and I heard the gobbler walking just behind her. If he appeared, he'd be just 35 yards away. I inched the shotgun into my shoulder and attempted to calm my rapidly beating heart.

Then, I heard a blast from another hunter's gun on the opposite side of the gobbler. I never saw the hen leave, but I watched the gobbler sail overhead.

I sat for several minutes and heard the other hunter walking over the hilltop. I expected him to show, but he never did. When all was quiet, I cautiously moved over the hill and looked for him. Apparently, he knew he had missed and left.

I had sat in that spot for more than 30 minutes, frequently called to the turkeys and heard no other calls. I believe the other hunter was attracted by the longbeard's constant gobbling, and had used the small strip-mined hills to stalk the bird.

I assumed he had settled for a long shot and missed — at least I hoped it was a clean miss.

Why the Ambush?

Ambushing a turkey is nothing new. Each year, folks kill turkeys by ambushing them. Some call to birds first but resort to stalks or ambushes if a gobbler doesn't cooperate. Others build their strategy around an ambush and never attempt to call in a bird.

But is there a right or wrong time to ambush a gobbler? Further, is ambushing a turkey ethical some, none or all of the time?

Joe Drake, a well-known hunter, champion caller and Realtree pro-staffer, admits he's ambushed several turkeys. However, he said they weren't preplanned. That is, calling to a gobbler is always his priority. Sometimes, if a gobbler won't respond to calling, it might be necessary to attempt an ambush. He recalled an area near his Georgia home where birds are called to so much that they're impossible to call in.

"There are several of us that hunt a particular military base," he said. "We take calling to the extreme, and these gobblers hear the best of the best calling. Some of these turkeys gobble their brains out, but after they hear calling, they don't say another word. Unless he (gobbler) sees another turkey walking around, he's going to go the other way. The only way you can kill one of these turkeys is to determine his travel route when he leaves. Then, you get in front of him and set up on him."

However, even after getting in front of a bird, Drake usually calls softly and avoids aggressive calls such as cutting, cackles and excited yelps. Stubborn birds sometimes show up without a sound.

I remember a similar situation in Kentucky. Through several days, every hunter who killed a turkey ambushed it. No gobblers worked to calling, and it seemed ambushing was the only way to fill tags.

Maybe unworkable turkeys are the products of education to calling. Drake mentioned a Texas ranch with pressured Rio Grande gobblers. After a group of birds comes to calling and sees one of their buddies killed, the rest become paranoid about hen talk. Then, hunters must ambush birds to kill one.

Merriam's are probably the least ambushed subspecies, probably because they eagerly respond to calling from long distances and often cross obstacles. However, ambushes are becoming more common in Eastern range, probably because of hunting pressure and the sheer difficulty of hunting the subspecies.

A Question of Ethics

The debate about ambush ethics has many facets. Some folks use blinds to hunt turkeys in a manner similar to deer hunting. They might spend hours waiting for a gobbler to walk within range but never call.

I don't blame anyone for choosing that ambush method — if that's what they want. I don't do it, mostly because it's not the way I enjoy spring hunting. I can't stand to sit and listen to a gobbler hammering on a hillside. If I hear a turkey, you can bet I'll move in to set up and call to the bird.

Another ambush involves stalking a turkey and sneaking into range without calling to the bird. A hunter sees or hears a gobbler, and then uses the terrain to sneak and crawl closer until he gets a shot.

Stalking isn't easy. Some consider this tactic unethical and unsportsmanlike, but who can deny that sneaking on a gobbler requires skill and woodsmanship? Most attempts probably fail, because a sharp-eyed gobbler will typically see a predator before it can get within 40 or 50 yards.

Nonetheless, stalking creates a dangerous situation. If another hunter is working the bird you're stalking, he might mistake your movement for the gobbler. However, I'd also consider you — the stalker — irresponsible.

Brian Lovett

Brian Lovett

That was certainly true when the hunter sneaked in and shot at the Indiana gobbler I was working. I was angry. I'd seen other hunters spook birds by attempting to get too close. However, when a hunter stalks and spooks a gobbler someone else is working, he has made a grave error.

The stalker I encountered prompts another point. Can a stalk or ambush lead to a missed or crippled bird? After all, a hunter might invest lots of time getting close only to have a bird see him and spook, tempting him to take an ill-advised shot.

What the Law Says

Pennsylvania prohibits hunters from stalking or ambushing spring gobblers. Richard Palmer, law-enforcement training supervisor, said the turkey hunting section of the state's 2001 Hunting Digest, says, "Hunting is by calling only and no stalking."

Palmer, who joined the force several years ago, said the regulation has been in effect as long as he can remember. He believes it was enacted after Pennsylvania reviewed hunting accidents and the incidents that led to them.

Also, Palmer said, the state's turkey population has increased, along with hunter numbers and hunting accidents. He believes many of the accidents were related to movement.

Despite the law, it can be difficult to prove that a hunter is stalking a turkey. Palmer said an officer would likely have to witness the stalk. Even then, he would have to prove the hunter wasn't just walking into an area or moving closer to begin calling.

Nonetheless, he said, the regulation makes a point: Don't stalk turkeys. Palmer said most hunters obey the law.

Conclusion

If not prohibited, stalking and ambushing a gobbler might be a viable option. If you face an obstinate longbeard that won't work to calling, the choice isn't right or wrong. It's just a matter of what appeals to you.

However, that's only true if you don't interfere with another hunter. Further, if you consider stalking a gobbler you haven't called to, think of the challenge you'll miss.

I won't consider an ambush regardless of the situation. If a gobbler doesn't fall for one calling tactic, I'll try another and another until the turkey is fooled or I'm whipped.

Again, it's a matter of choice.

Dangerous Games

Regardless of your opinion about the ethics of ambushing a turkey, consider another factor before planning a stalk.

Sneaking on a gobbler is dangerous. Imagine that another hunter is calling to the turkey. The bird answers, and minutes later, the caller sees movement near where the bird just gobbled. Although hunters should identify their target before shooting, an irresponsible hunter might mistake the stalker for a turkey.

Consider some other guidelines:
- Always try to call in a gobbler before attempting an ambush.
- Never attempt an ambush when you know another hunter is in the area. Assume you'll never know for sure if another hunter is nearby.
- Always listen for another hunter working a bird you're considering ambushing. If you suspect someone is working the bird, locate another turkey.
- If you can't call in a turkey, try to circle in front of the turkey and wait for him to come.
- Make sure you know the regulations regarding stalking or ambushing a turkey.

— John Trout Jr. is an accomplished turkey and deer hunter from southern Indiana.

CHAPTER 10

No Brakes

I really shouldn't have gone hunting that morning, but it was turkey season, darn it. In fact, it was Wisconsin's final turkey period, and I had one more chance to hunt my home state — one more chance to hear that longbeard gobble. I just couldn't slam the brakes on spring. I know you'd agree.

■ *BRIAN LOVETT*

At the time, it made perfect sense. It was 1:50 a.m., and I had propped my camouflaged, sleep-deprived body in the truck and headed southwest. With the CD player cranked and jumbo coffee mug at the ready, I started the 3-hour drive to Wisconsin's coulee country.

My gun, still caked with mud from that belly-crawl in Missouri, was thrown in the truck bed. My boots, hardened from numerous soakings and dryings, and leaky thanks to multiple ridges, hollows and swamps, had been thrown in the passenger seat. Mouth calls? Check. Glass call? In the vest. Cap? Oh yeah, it was on my head. Binoculars. Crap. I'd have to do without them.

As I left town and hit the highway, my eyes started to glaze. Groan. Sleep would have been nice. After all, it was May 16, and I had already "endured" two months of early mornings and hard walking. Plus, the fish were biting, and a cast-iron skillet full of walleye fillets seemed mighty appealing. Then my conscience kicked in, reminding me about that ratty lawn, untended garden and unpainted bathroom.

But man, what's a guy to do? It was turkey season, darn it. In fact, it was Wisconsin's final turkey period, and I had one more chance to hunt my home state — one more chance to hear that longbeard gobble. I just couldn't slam the brakes on spring. I knew you'd understand.

Stumbling In

I was supposed to meet my host, Jay Greene of Mount Sterling, Wis., at 4:45 a.m. Of course, I was late, and it didn't help that I dodged deer throughout my drive through the hills and valleys of southwestern Wisconsin.

At 5 a.m., I stopped at Greene's house, where his wife, Lisa, told me he had just left. He wasn't hunting far away, though, so I took quick directions and ambled north on the gravel town road. Five minutes later, I pulled into a field road and greeted Greene and his father, Jim.

"Hey, you made it," Greene said quietly. "Just in time for the gobbling."

"Barely," I replied, trying to shake off the fog in my head. "I hope I didn't hold you guys up."

"Naw, we're just going to hunt right over here," he said, pointing to a deep woods that bordered a hilltop alfalfa field. "You can go anywhere down here on the other side. There have been four longbeards hanging out in that area, and no one has hunted it in five weeks."

That sounded just fine to me, so I grabbed my gear and traipsed down a fence line bordering an old cut cornfield toward the huge timber-rimmed ravine below.

Halfway there, I stopped on a high point and listened intently for gobbles. Birds had started hammering in the distance, but I knew there had to be more nearby. The area just looked too good.

I waited for several minutes, reminding myself to be patient. And sure enough, after enduring uncertainty for as long as possible, a bird sounded off in the woods straight down the fence line. Other gobblers quickly joined in, and I made a bee line toward them.

After reaching the woods, I crept along the edge, trying to get a better fix on the first longbeard. He had shut up momentarily, but I was sure I was in his neighborhood.

"Gaaarrrroble!"

I hit the dirt. I was more than in the neighborhood; I was at the front door. The bird was roosted in a huge oak just below the ridgetop about 70 yards from where I stood. And from what I heard, he was alone — and hot.

Quietly, I slipped into the woods and found a good set-up tree. I was about 50 yards from the turkey and 20 steps from a small terrain rise below the ridgetop. The bird would likely fly down toward the ridge, I reasoned, which would put him in range. One cluck would likely do it.

Things were just too perfect.

Hide and Seek

I clucked once on my glass call, and the bird gobbled hard — so close that I could see the leaves in his roost tree shake.

"All right, good enough," I thought. "Stick tight and be ready for flydown."

I tree-yelped once or twice after that and then put the call away. The longbeard gobbled intermittently for the next 15 minutes but abruptly shut up as light began to filter into the deep woods.

"Any second now," I thought.

On cue, I heard heavy wingbeats and caught flashes of a dark streak as the big bird pitched straight down in front of me. He was probably 45 yards away below the rise, and he knew right where I was.

I yelped softly on my mouth call, and the gobbler hammered back. My shotgun barrel shook as I peered down the rib, expecting to see a snowball-white head pop up at any second. The turkey took his time, though.

Drumming filled the woods as the longbeard drifted to the left just below the ridge. Slowly, I shifted my body with the bird, keeping the gun pointed toward the sound. I clucked and yelped sparingly, but the bird refused to gobble. He was close to that "hen," and all "she" would get from that point was his subtle love talk.

The standoff continued for several minutes, and doubt crept into my mind.

"Where is he?" I thought. "He's got to be right there, but why won't he pop up to take a look?"

Getting impatient, I yelped again on my diaphragm.

"Gaaaarrrrrroble!"

That rat. He had drifted down the ridgeline to my left and was probably 75 yards away. The old boy had come as far as he would, and he wasn't about to charge in to that noisy hen. She — I — would have to go to him.

I called again and got the bird to gobble twice more. By then, however, he was on his way down the ridge, heading toward greener pastures. The sure thing had turned into yet another butt-whipping from an old gobbler.

I was ticked but remained optimistic. Hey, it wasn't even 6 a.m. yet. I might not kill that gobbler, but I'd sure try.

Walking to the edge of the woods, I grabbed my glass call and bore down on the striker, ringing yelps and cutting off the hillsides. Two gobbles echoed back from over the hill, and shrill hen yelps followed.

So that's where that bad bird was headed. There were turkeys in the cut cornfield.

Cutting a swath through the dew on the alfalfa, I half-sprinted to the hilltop. If those birds were going to lead me on a chase, I'd sure oblige and follow.

Giveaway Gobble and the Creep

After reading the hilltop fence line, I stopped to survey the field. At first, I saw nothing, but I knew it was misleading. The cornfield had many twists, turns and dips: perfect terrain breaks for hiding turkeys.

I yelped on my mouth call. Nothing. Then, I cutt on the glass. Still nothing. I was stuck. Until I pinpointed where those birds were, I couldn't move without risking disaster.

"They're right there," I thought, reassuring myself. "Be patient, and keep after them."

For once, my own advice worked. After a few more calling sequences, a lone gobble responded from a hidden low spot in the field. The gobbler and, I assumed, the other birds were probably 100 yards down the hill near an island of brush surrounding a dead cherry tree. Better yet, if I cut down the fence line and then slipped along the edge of the woods, the terrain would cover my approach.

I covered the ground in about five minutes, and then was faced with one final dilemma. I had to traverse about 40 yards of open ground from the woods edge to brushy island, which was atop a small rise in the field. Laying my gun on the ground before me, I began the slow creep toward the cherry tree, constantly scanning the rise for any movement.

As I approached the brush, I painstakingly eased my head up for a look. Movement about 25 yards beyond the cherry tree caught my eye, and before I realized what was occurring, I was staring at a strutter dogging a hen as she rapidly walked from right to left.

I eased back down and crawled to the left of the brush. I only had to reach the tiny crest, and I'd have a shot at the gobbler. Suddenly, though, I froze.

Another gobbler had topped the ridge about 55 yards to my left. He glared at me suspiciously and craned his neck.

"It's finished," I thought. "I'll be busted before I can get closer."

However, I must have seen him soon enough, because the bird resumed strutting, disappeared over the rise and apparently joined the others. The hunt was back on.

I crawled as far as I dared to the rise and peered through the weeds. About 35 yards away, two gobblers strutted over a hen while two more longbeards walked nervously around them. I yelped softly on my diaphragm, and a raucous gobble filled the air.

"This is it," I thought, settling my shotgun's sights on the closest bird.

I yelped again, and another bird hammered back. The second longbeard in line raised his head high to look, and I shot.

Instantly, I sprang to my feet and sprinted to the scene. Turkeys flew everywhere, and for a second, I wondered whether I had missed. However, a flopping black blob told me differently. I whispered a quick thanks and put my hands around the gobbler's feet. The dandy 3-year-old had 1 1/8-inch spurs and a 11 1/4-inch beard. He'd done his share of breeding, too, because his breastbone was bare of feathers, and he weighed just 17-1/2 pounds.

Statistics aside, the bird had topped off the long season. I threw him over my shoulder and trudged up the hill, confident I had made the final addition to my box of spring memories — or so I thought.

The Lord Smiles Again

At the field road, Greene greeted me with a broad grin.

"Hey, that's not bad," he said. "I guess that makes getting up at 1:30 a.m. worthwhile."

It had, I sheepishly acknowledged. And how had Greene and his father done?

"One gobble, and that was it," he said. "But I heard them tearing it up down by you."

I was almost embarrassed. Greene and I were relative strangers, yet he had invited me to hunt his land after a mutual friend introduced us. Then, I'd stumbled into success while my benefactor had experienced a tough early morning.

"Well, this place sure has lots of birds," I said. "You guys will kill one yet today."

"We're sure going to try," he replied. "Want to come with us?"

I couldn't pass up that offer. After snapping a few photos, I joined Jay Greene, Jim Greene and Jeff Redman, Greene's brother-in-law, as they drove to another farm. The sun was high and getting hot, but there was still plenty of morning remaining.

After greeting the farmer, we set out on a field road for a hightop pasture. Redman had killed a gobbler on the property during Wisconsin's first season, and he knew the area well.

"The birds seem to like to hang out in that corner or just over that rise by those woods," he said.

And, as predicted, two birds immediately responded to my third series of yelps from the edge of a woods just over the tall rise. We scrambled to a nearby tree line and set up. Redman and Jim Greene found trees on the field edge, and Jay Greene and I sat 40 yards behind them to call. Meanwhile, the gobblers continued to fire up — and they were moving.

When everyone was ready, I cutt on my glass call, and the longbeards jumped all over it. By then, they had moved to the crest of the hill and seemed to be closing fast.

I continued calling, mixing plaintive yelps with clucks, and the birds gobbled at almost everything. Even better, they never stopped to strut, but moved steadily along the hilltop road to a corner of woods to our right. They came into view briefly, legs pumping and beards swinging, and then, turned and started down the edge.

Fearful that the toms would come into the woods to our calling instead of to Jim Greene and Redman, I turned my glass call toward the field and tried to cast my yelps toward

the open. I don't know if it made a difference, but the birds headed right to the shooters. Seconds later, I heard drumming, saw flashes of two white heads and heard a wonderful sound:

"Bam-bam!"

Both turkeys folded and went down, and Redman and Jim Greene raced to claim them. It had been a classic double, and the gobblers had been hotter than any I'd worked all season. Further, the toms displayed light, almost bronze-phase coloration, and featured bragging-sized beards and spurs.

And with that, I knew my season was complete. Nothing would top that hunt.

And That's Why

The rest of that day, we took pictures and talked turkey hunting. Greene, Redman and I ate breakfast at Redman's tavern, and then they introduced me to the rest of their crew.

We sat in Greene's yard late into the afternoon, each hunter telling his story from that morning and talking about turkeys past and future. And we drank beer, ran a few calls and plotted strategy for the next day.

When I left, I didn't feel so tired. And during the next few days, the grass got trimmed, the garden was tended and I even caught a walleye or two.

In hindsight, I made the right decision by going turkey hunting that morning. Really, it was the only decision I could have made.

I knew you'd understand.

— Brian Lovett served as editor of Turkey & Turkey Hunting *from August 1995 through January 2002. Currently, he is the editor of* Bass Pro Shops' Outdoor World *magazine.*

CHAPTER 11

Turkey Hunting Safety Series Part I: An Ounce of Prevention

Turkey hunting accidents are the result of how hunters react to meeting each other. Imagine being pelted with BBs in the arms, face or chest. It doesn't take much description to make even the toughest stomach shudder.

■ JENNIFER WEST

Turkey hunters expect certain things: a cold spring morning, the lush green of new leaves and undergrowth, and the warmth of the midmorning

Brian Lovett

sun. The sport is about interaction. We expect to freeze in midstep at the sound of a gobble, sneak into position before dawn, and listen to hens just over the crest of a ridge. That's why we go; just to be there when the woods awaken.

However, you might also encounter the unexpected. With so many hunters in the woods each spring and fall, accidents and shooting incidents occur.

The Fall 2000 issue of *Turkey & Turkey Hunting* contained a safety survey designed to determine why turkey hunters are wounded and sometimes killed each year. We hope the results revealed here will in some way decrease the dangerous circumstances that sometimes occur.

The Results

Almost 800 readers responded to the survey. The average respondent was 49 years old, had hunted turkeys for more than 15 years, and spends about 74 hours hunting turkeys in spring and 30 hours hunting turkeys in fall.

The largest portion of respondents came from Pennsylvania, New York, Wisconsin and Missouri, respectively, with a fairly even sprinkling throughout other states. And, as you might expect for a survey about safety, 66 percent said they're very concerned with turkey hunting safety.

That raises an interesting question. What does turkey hunting safety mean? Is it a simple matter of knowing how to use a compass, avoid hypothermia and safely carry a firearm? Are turkey hunting's accidents preventable? Are they something we can train new hunters to deal with?

Actually, the *T&TH* survey found that most accidents occur when hunters encounter one another, when they're unaware of who is in the woods around them, and when they approach the sound of a turkey thinking a gobbler is strutting just over the hill — when it's really a camouflaged hunter.

Cause and Effect

Interaction, and sometimes interference, from other hunters is unavoidable. When hunting on public land, where hunter numbers burgeon in spring, it's ridiculous to believe you are alone in the woods.

The scary part for many hunters — and survey respondents involved in accidents — is that turkey hunters don't remain still. Turkey hunting involves interaction, mimicking and concealment. It's a game of fooling a tom, and sometimes that role-playing fools fellow hunters.

About 58 percent of survey respondents reported that they had been approached by other hunters when calling or using decoys. Many said that had happened several times.

"In two instances, hunters came to my hen calls ... I had to yell, 'Stop,' and I feared they might have shot at me or my decoys," wrote a reader from Pennsylvania.

Another reader from New York had a similar experience.

"On two occasions," he wrote, "I was approached by another hunter who was tracking my calls."

Those represent typical responses to our survey, establishing that contact with other hunters is common. That type of response also established that hunters are commonly stalked and mistaken as turkeys even though most hunters are using hen calls when only gobblers can be shot. Nearly 93 percent of our survey respondents use hen sounds while calling to or locating turkeys, and 41 percent use gobbler calls. Many of the write-in responses indicated that those who stalked a hen sound believed that a gobbler was close at hand.

Now, the question of safety comes into play. How do hunters react to such circumstances? Thankfully, many follow the guidelines vigilantly taught in hunter-education classes: Always verify what you are shooting at. Being aware of your target is the only solution to avoiding an accident.

However, there were enough examples of injuries and people shooting at unknown targets to make average turkey hunters tremble. Almost 9 percent of survey respondents had been shot at, and about 2 percent had been hit or injured by careless shots.

Those who were shot have horror stories to prove that safety is a big deal.

Too Close for Comfort

Imagine being pelted with BBs in the arms, face or chest. It doesn't take much description to make even the toughest stomach shudder.

"The guy I was hunting with saw movement and fired," wrote a reader from Pennsylvania. "I was hit in the head and upper body with 15 to 18 pellets. I lost my left eye."

Another reader was approached by a 15-year-old boy who heard a tom the reader was calling to. The boy ran across a pasture and through the woods, saw movement behind a tree, and shot the reader in the head, back and side. Dozens of pellets hit the man, causing permanent kidney and liver damage. He still carries 30 to 35 pellets in his body.

The stories continue: collapsed lungs, pellets lodged in skull plates and permanent damage — from preventable accidents.

In those situations, and others that resulted in no injuries, the No. 1 combination of events was that one hunter was calling while another hunter stalked what he perceived to be a turkey. Also, most of the incidents occurred between hunters who didn't know each other. Only 15 percent of respondents involved in potentially dangerous hunting incidents knew each other. Also, almost 78 percent didn't know there was another hunter in the area.

Prevention

Many respondents suggested that hunter-education classes were the key to decreasing accidents. Others said wearing blaze orange at all times would do the trick. Still others suggested tagging your hunting area with orange flags or ribbons to alert other hunters to your setup.

After the 1990 and 1991 fall season, Pennsylvania was forced to examine such options. The state experienced its worst period for accidents, with 75 accidents in two seasons, five of which were fatal.

The state implemented a blaze-orange law for fall and spring seasons, and saw a dramatic decrease in accidents the preceding fall. Turkey hunting accidents plunged to six, none of which were fatal.

Brian Lovett

Was that a result of abundant press coverage and increased awareness about dangerous situations, or was blaze orange really effective?

In our survey, 98 percent of respondents said they are fully camouflaged when in the woods. Almost 19 percent use blaze orange to distinguish their presence while hunting, and almost 44 percent use blaze orange while moving through the woods. Interestingly, respondents involved in a shooting incident used blaze orange more frequently while hunting. Perhaps that's a result of their accidents.

When Turkey Hunting Accidents Occur

John Vanover, of Clintonwood, Va., was experiencing a typical fall turkey hunt in 1998. He had set up against a tree, and had been calling periodically for about 20 to 30 minutes when another hunter stalked his calling. The other hunter crawled on his belly toward Vanover. When the man was 67 feet away, he fired at what he perceived was a turkey. Eighteen pellets hit Vanover. Three were almost fatal, coming within a fraction of an inch of his chest and brain.

Vanover needed three operations to remove four pellets from behind his ear and over his eye.

"My life has been a nightmare since this happened," he wrote. "I am so nervous, and I jump at any loud noise. The thing that has been taken away from me that I miss the most is my peace of mind.

"I don't know if I can ever go hunting again. Maybe someday this fear will gradually leave me."

For Ray Eriksen, the physical nightmare of a turkey hunting accident has been even worse. On May 16, 1987, Eriksen began wandering his property after a slow morning of hunting. He had seen a vehicle earlier, but hadn't given it much thought. At about 9 a.m., he stood to stretch, gave one last series of yelps on his box call and headed down the hill.

A hunter was set up at the bottom of the hill, and fired a load of No. 4 shot at Eriksen after mistaking his movement for a turkey. More than 90 of the 120 pellets hit him, penetrating his skull and side. He was left with a permanent limp, problems with his right hand and epilepsy.

For the rest of his life, Eriksen must take antiseizure medication. He was out of work for almost a year, and was unable to drive for years until his medication was properly regulated. That medication eventually caused severe bone-mass loss, leaving his bones very brittle.

In an attempt to prevent more bone loss, Eriksen's doctor switched his medication. However, in another chapter of the

Highlights from *Turkey & Turkey Hunting's* Safety Survey

What do you believe caused or contributed most to the accident/incident?

27.3%	Stalking or sneaking
22.7%	Calling (hen sounds)
15.3%	Trespassing
12.7%	Other
9.4%	Failure to identify target
4.2%	Calling (gobbler sounds)
4.2%	Failure to identify beyond target
2.6%	Decoys
1.6%	Improper set up
0%	Accidental discharge, or misfire

What did you know about the other hunter involved in the accident/incident?

77.5%	I did not know another hunter was in the area
14.0%	I knew another hunter was in the area, but I was not hunting with him
5.5%	Trespassing
3%	Other

domino-like story, that medication caused a heart attack. Eriksen was only 47 years old.

Since then, his health has improved, but the future is still a great unknown.

"All of the pain and expense could have been avoided had I not gone down that hill that morning," he wrote. "All of it could have been avoided had the shooter clearly identified his target. You must remember that you cannot recall the shot once the trigger has been pulled."

With that statement, Eriksen nails the point of turkey hunting safety: Know your target. It's up to you to be a defensive hunter and a wise one.

"I hope everyone who reads your magazine reads the results of your survey," Eriksen wrote. "If it can save one person from going through the pain and heartache this incident put my family through, it is worth printing."

Conclusion

Every time you enter the turkey woods, there's the potential for accidents. Hunters can set up on the same bird, wander between a bird and another hunter, stalk another hunter's calling or approach a decoy setup thinking it's the real thing. Ultimately, however, it comes down to identifying a target. It's such a basic concept — but such a necessary one.

Although stated often in hunter-education literature, these tips deserve repetition:

✔ Positively identify your target. Be sure the shot path to the bird and beyond is safe.

✔ Make your position known to other hunters by using orange bands or ribbon.

✔ Assume every noise and movement is another hunter.

✔ Protect your back. Select a large tree or rock while setting up and calling. Hunt in open woods.

✔ Shout "Stop!" to alert approaching hunters.

✔ Eliminate red, white, blue and black, which are found on mature gobblers, from your clothing.

✔ Be careful when using decoys.

Be a defensive hunter. Assume other hunters are around you, and be a safe shooter.

It will help eliminate the unexpected.

— Jennifer West served as managing editor of Turkey & Turkey Hunting *for several years. Currently, she is the managing editor of* Bass Pro Shops' Outdoor World *magazine.*

Brian Lovett

CHAPTER 12

Turkey Hunting Safety Series Part II: A Pound of Cure

Turkey hunting is much safer than most sports, such as billiards, soccer and tennis. So why are hunters so concerned about safety issues?

■ JENNIFER WEST

What is safer than playing billiards, soccer and tennis yet attracts about 1.76 million participants?

You've probably guessed that the answer is turkey hunting, seeing as how this is a turkey hunting magazine. And, you're right.

According to the National Wild Turkey Federation, 52 turkey hunting incidents were reported during Spring 2000, averaging 2.95 injuries per 100,000 participants.

That compares with an average of 10.2 billiard accidents per 100,000 players, 13.7 soccer-related emergency room visits and 200.5 tennis-related accidents. In all, that makes turkey hunting look like a pretty safe sport.

So why are hunters so concerned about safety? Why are there task forces meeting in closed rooms, discussing how to reduce shotgun accidents? Why are hunters so adamant about teaching up-and-coming sportsmen the dos and don'ts of woods etiquette? You don't hear about billiards training or soccer-safety courses, do you?

Those are easy questions to answer. What happens in the woods generally isn't an accident. Hunter-inflicted injuries or fatalities happen because someone was careless, trespassing or taking a risky shot. Injury in the turkey woods generally happens because of a decision someone made, and that is why many agencies and natural-resources departments have coined the phrase "hunting incident" to replace "hunting accident."

Also, these incidents tend to be traumatic. In the March 2001 *Turkey & Turkey Hunting*, we ran the first article in this safety series, which addressed some of the life-altering incidents that have occurred because of careless decisions. It's difficult to forget the picture of John Vanover, who took several pellets to his head and upper torso. It's hard to forget the story of Ray Eriksen, who now has epilepsy from pellets that penetrated his skull.

Because such incidents are preventable yet so traumatic, it isn't surprising that turkey hunting safety is a serious matter.

In this, the final segment of *T&TH's* turkey hunting safety series, we'll zoom out to look at the big picture — what state departments and national organizations are doing to promote safety, and what their goals and visions are for turkey hunters.

Season Structure

Wherever you choose to hunt turkeys this spring, you must acknowledge the season determined by the state. Many season dates are based heavily on hunter satisfaction.

Wisconsin represents an interesting model. The prime objective of the state's turkey management program is to maintain a secure turkey population capable of supporting a safe, high-quality hunt with reasonable hunter success. Sound demanding? Well, the state has succeeded so far. Wisconsin boasts a low accident rate with relatively good feedback from hunters.

Wisconsin has a lottery system for a series of six five-day seasons. Depending on landowner status and luck of the draw, you receive a tag for your preferred zone and time period. Wisconsin bases the number of permits on hunter

satisfaction and interference determined by hunter questionnaires.

The number of permits is also based off a predetermined concentration of three hunters per square mile of wooded land in a specific time period. The Wisconsin Department of Natural Resources experimented with this number when the turkey population began increasing in Wisconsin and extending northward.

From 1989 to 1991, the state conducted an experiment in Vernon County in southwestern Wisconsin to determine hunter perceptions of a safe, quality hunt. The state also wanted to determine landowner tolerance of hunters, which

is where the figure of three hunters per square mile of wooded land originated.

Fall hunters in the experimental zone accepted a higher density of hunters, probably because they expected to encounter greater interference from bow-hunters, small-game hunters and other turkey hunters.

By keeping hunter numbers low, the state has maintained its safety record. Since turkey hunting began in Wisconsin, the number of accidents per 100,000 permits has averaged 3.4 during spring and 5.4 during fall. That compares with a nationwide average of 8.3 in spring and 9.3 in fall from 1990 to 1992.

The state allows room for change in hunter-concentration numbers.

"It's just a benchmark number," said Keith Warnke, Wisconsin's upland wildlife specialist. "That number is constantly reviewed because hunters seem to tolerate more interaction."

Warnke said some areas continually don't come close to the benchmark number. Those areas have plenty of room for growth.

Michigan also works on a variation of the lottery system. Field biologists determine the social and biological carrying capacity of a zone, which establishes permit numbers.

Brian Lovett

"We spend a lot of effort to mail surveys," said wildlife biologist Al Stewart.

Michigan shoots for a 70 percent hunter satisfaction rate based on extensive hunter surveys, which, like Wisconsin, has also resulted in minimal accidents.

However, Michigan has added a little variety to the equation. The last periods of the season are open, and, as of this year, have been expanded to May 7.

"Knowledgeable hunters view it as an excellent hunt," Stewart said. "Others viewed it as a mosquito hunt. After a lot of comment, we expanded it."

Lottery systems like those in Wisconsin and Michigan tend to be used in states that are newer to turkey hunting. Warnke said the open-permit system used in states like Pennsylvania and Missouri was put in place before turkey hunting became so popular.

In those states, hunters sometimes encounter an "opening-day" mentality on the first day of the season. Does that make turkey hunting in open-permit states unsafe? Not necessarily, but it can increase the amount of hunter interference and the potential for accidents.

Educated Minds

Perhaps the greatest element of turkey hunting safety is education. With all the millions of brochures the NWTF

Highlights from the Safety Survey

How do you rate turkey hunting safety in the state where you hunt?

47.2%	Very safe
48.0%	Somewhat safe
3.8%	Somewhat unsafe
1.0%	Very unsafe

How concerned are you about turkey hunting safety?

66.0%	Very concerned
28.6%	Somewhat concerned
5.4%	Not concerned

hands out and the thousands of safety courses held throughout the country each year, it is almost impossible not to know what safety means.

"It's very hard to enforce safety," said Gunn. "The best way is through education."

In the *T&TH* survey, almost 60 percent of the respondents had taken a hunter-education course, and of

Brian Lovett

those, almost 50 percent said a portion of the class was dedicated to turkey hunting safety.

Of course, most basic safety elements hold true for turkey hunting: Always treat any gun as if it were loaded, and be sure of your target and beyond.

"In the case of an accident, unless the shot was self-inflicted, it was because of the shooter's failure to positively identify his target," said Tim Lawhern, hunter education coordinator for the Wisconsin DNR and president-elect of the International Hunter Education Association.

During a shooting investigation, Lawhern asks the shooter if he was sure of his target.

"An all-too often comment is, 'No,'" said Lawhern. "They didn't know how to identify a turkey."

Ultimately, no matter how much state organizations monitor hunter numbers and national organizations promote

safety, the responsibility lies with the hunter. With more hunters in the woods than before, it is necessary to think defensively. Be aware of your surroundings and the people on the land you hunt, and always identify your target.

Turkey hunting might be one of the safest sports, but it's only because turkey hunters are safety-conscious. Keep your head on straight in while hunting. Identify your target, and don't make the mistake of thinking you're immune to accidents.

— Jennifer West served several years as managing editor of Turkey & Turkey Hunting.

Is Pennsylvania's Blaze-Orange Law the Answer to Safety?

When Pennsylvania initiated the first-ever blaze orange requirement for turkey hunting, sportsmen took notice. The law came on the heels of Pennsylvania's worst-ever year for hunting accidents. In the 1990 fall season, 38 hunters were shot of which three were fatalities. In the 1991 fall season, 37 hunters were shot and two were fatalities. That spring, 19 more accidents occurred in the turkey woods, which attracted attention from wildlife biologists and sportsmen.

The result? Pennsylvania placed a 250-inch blaze orange requirement on fall hunters and a 100-inch requirement on spring hunters. The next year, accidents dropped to six in fall and were cut in half in Spring 1992.

However, although the blaze-orange law seemed to dramatically decrease the number of accidents in Pennsylvania, the National Wild Turkey Federation did not approve. The NWTF believes that although blaze-orange contributes to hunter safety, it is not the most effective way to hunt. Brad Gunn, wildlife biologist at the NWTF and liaison to the International Hunter Education Association, said there is no firm evidence that blaze orange makes turkey hunting safer.

"People will not adhere to the use of blaze orange because it cuts down on their chances of killing a turkey," he said.

Gunn said that in a 1997 report filed by an NWTF task force, blaze orange cannot be universally applied to all types of hunting. In that report, the group stated its opposition to the mandated use of hunter orange for spring turkey hunting.

The reasons include:

✔ Turkeys can see color, so blaze orange reduces a hunter's chance of success.

✔ Small patches of hunter orange have been identified as contributing factors in some hunter injury scenarios. The task force report cites a 1999 spring turkey accident in New York in which a hunter was shot when he flashed the orange lining of his hat to alert another hunter of his presence.

✔ In low light, blaze orange can appear red, which is one of a gobbler's primary colors.

✔ Hunter acceptance and compliance is a concern because, in general, spring turkey hunters prefer camouflage rather than hunter orange.

Opponents of mandatory blaze-orange argue that education and awareness could have been the underlying causes of the accident reduction in Pennsylvania.

In the safety survey conducted by *Turkey & Turkey Hunting*, 19 percent of the almost 800 respondents said they use blaze orange to distinguish their presence while hunting. Nearly 44 percent of respondents said they use blaze orange while walking to a new location. For comparison, 12 percent of the survey respondents were from Pennsylvania, illustrating that blaze-orange is being used in states where it is not required.

What does the NWTF recommend for safety? Full camouflage. As stated by the NWTF Safety Task Force, being fully camouflaged decreases any confusion that could result from noticing a swatch of color in the woods.

In the *T&TH* survey, 98 percent of respondents stated they prefer to use full camouflage.

CHAPTER 13

The Small Hours

Finally, you've reached your listening post. Now, as traces of silver tinge the eastern sky, the wait begins.

■ BRIAN LOVETT

They are the small minutes, when time slowly ticks away as you wait for the first gobble of the season. These moments won't be the most exciting or memorable you spend in the turkey woods this spring, but you'll never feel as much adrenaline, awareness and anticipation as during these fleeting ticks of the clock.

Whether we start the season in Alabama, Missouri or New York, turkey hunters share this experience. You wake up before the alarm, perhaps spurred by breakfast cooking down the hallway or the noise of a hunting partner shuffling in the darkness. You're up but not alert. After all, it's opening day, and your body isn't used to turkey hours yet.

You fumble through your vest, making sure everything is in order. Where did you put that friction call? Is one of your strikers missing? No, there it is. Hmm, those new boots seem a bit tight. No doubt, you'll break them in during the ensuing days. Time to double-check your facemask and gloves. Yes, you're ready after all.

It's time for breakfast. Perhaps you're at a Southern lodge, where the cook has prepared heaping piles of scrambled eggs and potatoes. Maybe you're at a cabin, where your buddy has again managed to cook the yolks too hard and spoil the coffee. Or, like many folks, you probably sit bleary-eyed at your kitchen table, wolfing down a quick bowl of cereal before it's time to hit the road.

The truck engine hums in the darkness as you wipe off the windows and make sure to stow your gun carefully. You check the sky through your windshield. A few clouds, but it looks to be a good gobbling morning. Cripes, you'd better get going. You're five minutes behind schedule, and you have a hike in front of you after you reach your hunting area.

At last, you're here. You grab your stuff and carefully ease the door shut so you don't disturb the landowners and turkeys. After a few steps through the dew-covered field, you're thankful you wore rubber boots. It's cold!

Now, where's that trail? Sure enough, that's it. You hike up the ridge toward the second finger, where you roosted two gobblers the previous night. A stick snaps beneath your feet, and you curse your clumsiness.

"Slow down," you whisper in the darkness. "You're acting like a rookie."

Finally, you've reached your listening post. Now, as traces of silver tinge the eastern sky, the wait begins.

Where will that gobble come from? How will you sneak into position? What will your first calling sequence be? It's been so long since last season. Will you even remember what to do? Of course you will. This isn't your first time. That doesn't make the wait easier, though.

Boy, it would be nice to have a hot-gobbling bird pitch down 20 yards in front of you, wouldn't it? You could cluck once, make the shot and be back at camp sipping coffee by 7:30 a.m. Yeah, that would be nice, but you realize you'll probably have to work hard and log some hours to kill a bird.

The stars are fading now, but the woods remain silent. Did you spook him? Was all your pre-season scouting a waste? Is it going to be one of those days?

There! There's a gobble, ringing loud and throaty through the woods. Man, he's close, and you know just the setup to begin calling. There he was again. He's hammering, and you're in perfect position.

You'd better get going, because that longbeard won't wait forever. The small minutes are finished for another year, and dawn will soon break, ushering in a new turkey season and the promise of memories to come.

— Brian Lovett *served as editor of* Turkey & Turkey Hunting *from August 1995 through January 2002. Currently, he is the editor of* Bass Pro Shops' Outdoor World *magazine.*

Brian Lovett

TIES THAT BIND

*O*ld snapshots reveal a lot about turkey hunting. Sure, you immediately notice the bird, fanned out on the ground, slung over someone's shoulder, or propped and displayed on a hunter's knee. But after further observation, you start to notice the folks and scenes in pictures more than the birds. And I think that reveals a lot about turkey hunting.

We've all been richly rewarded by hearing gobbling, watching longbeards strut and overcoming seemingly great odds to find success. But as our turkey hunting careers progress, we begin to realize the many attachments and bonds we've formed during our days afield.

A fellow hunter easily becomes a brother in arms. First turkey hunts spawn lifelong friendships. Days afield prompt memories of those who came before us. And a hardwood ridge or Southern river bottom become more than turkey habitat — they're sacred ground.

If this seems sappy or melancholy, don't worry. This section won't get too maudlin. Hopefully, it will just help you recognize the greatest reward turkey hunting offers — the deep ties to each other and the land around us.

■ BRIAN LOVETT

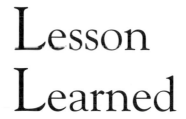

CHAPTER 1

Lesson Learned

My shotgun is halfway to my shoulder, my mouth is hanging open, and I'm a lot smarter than I was 30 seconds ago.

■ RON LEYS

The year was 1983, and we were even dumber than we are now—not about the opposite sex but about hunting turkeys.

My home state of Wisconsin was once full of superb turkey hunters, American Indian and non-Indian. The problem was they were so good at their trade that one of them shot the state's last wild turkey in the 1870s. A century later, wild turkeys were imported from Missouri and released in southwestern Wisconsin. By then, those old turkey hunters had been pushing up daisies for many years.

An Astonishing Permit

So now it's 1983, and turkeys are flourishing, multiplying, gobbling and yelping out there. The Wisconsin Department of Natural Resources decides it's time to turn hunters loose on turkeys, or at least some hunters on some turkeys. After all, that was the original idea.

By now, there's been lots of publicity about this turkey reintroduction, and plenty of hunters are interested. So the DNR devises a lottery and offers about 1,000 permits to shoot gobblers. About 10,000 hunters apply, so one in 10 gets lucky. One of the hunters, to my astonishment, is me.

OK, now some of us have licenses to hunt turkeys. The

problem is we don't know where to hunt, and we don't have a clue how to do it — not a clue.

Well, problems are solvable, right? And the DNR is going to help us solve them, as always. First, to address the how-to, they set up turkey hunting workshops throughout the state and invite lucky permit holders.

I attend one of the workshops. It's nice, with videos, lectures and calling demonstrations — until a guy in the audience asks the experts on stage whether any of them has ever hunted turkeys. None have. Uh-oh. I think these guys are as dumb as me.

But I have a license and a shotgun, and I bought a box call at the workshop. I'm as ready as I'm going to be. Now, to find a place.

I read the DNR had bought a big piece of wild land somewhere north of Wauzeka in Crawford County, but I don't know exactly how to get there. So, I go to the experts: the guys at the county highway garage. Of course, they know where it is. And, of course, they tell me.

To the Chase

So here I am on the first morning of the first turkey season in Wisconsin's modern history, sitting against a tree on a hillside overlooking the Kickapoo River, making my box call make sounds I hope resemble the yelps of a horny hen. Of course, I have never heard a real hen turkey — horny or not — so I have no idea whether I'm doing this right.

From time to time, I hear a gobble in the woods. I answer. But after a couple of hours, it becomes obvious the gobbling toms know whether I'm doing this right. The answer is "no."

This continues for several mornings, until I'm on the last day of my season. Things are looking a little desperate. So I go to Plan B. If the toms won't come to me, I'll go to them. I'll sneak up on them.

Sure enough, I hear gobbling across a valley and up a steep hillside. I slowly skulk through the woods, cradling the old 12-gauge, ready for action.

As I approach the top of the rise, out of breath from the long climb, I hear sounds like 100 squirrels scratching in dry leaves. I ease over the top and there, right in front of me, is a picture out of *Sports Afield*.

A huge tom is strutting back and forth, with its tail spread, wings drooping, feathers shaking and blood-red head thrown back. In front of the gobbler, a half-dozen hens are scratching for acorns, paying no attention to Mr. Magnificent or me.

So I slowly begin to raise my gun.

Then, a hen races over from the left, putting at the top of her lungs: "He's got a gun! He's got a gun!"

Now all I see is turkey fannies disappearing through the woods at about 400 mph. My shotgun is halfway to my shoulder, my mouth is hanging open, and I'm a lot smarter than I was 30 seconds ago.

I have just learned you can't sneak up on a turkey.

Another Difficult Lesson

Some things in life must be learned the hard way — by experience, as they say. One such lesson is that you can't sneak up on a turkey and expect to shoot him. Another is that you can't raise the big bettor $5, and then hope to draw a seven-card to an inside straight and expect to win at poker.

Some day I'll tell you how I learned that.

— *Ron Leys is a free-lance writer from southwestern Wisconsin.*

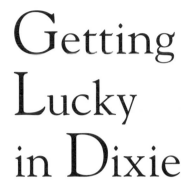

CHAPTER 2

Getting Lucky in Dixie

I was certainly out of my element, but this turkey hunt reconfirmed an adage I use in the deer woods: Patience and perseverance don't usually go unrewarded.

■ *DANIEL E. SCHMIDT*

My knee bobbed uncontrollably as I tried to steady the shotgun toward the oncoming gobbler. I could sense the seriousness of the moment when my guide, Brian Ross, whispered sternly, "Whatever you do, don't move."

I took a breath, exhaled, and buried my jawbone tight and low on the gun's stock while peering down the barrel.

Ross whispered more tips as he watched a group of hens pick their way toward us along the edge of a cotton field. A steady rain drowned his voice, however, so I tried to focus on the one opening in the brush I could shoot through.

The shotgun grew heavy and swayed in small circles. I hoped these hens would soon have male companions.

This was my first turkey hunting trip, and it was the first time I had seen wild turkeys up close. Although turkeys are abundant near my central Wisconsin home, I had yet to receive a permit to hunt them.

As I watched the birds step by 17 yards away, I could tell something caught Ross' attention.

"Gobbler!" he whispered.

The rain was running steadily off my balloap and down my neck, but I continued to bear down on the shotgun.

"Just like a whitetail," I told myself. "Just pick a spot and aim."

In seconds, I caught the bird's movement to my right. The tom entered the opening, stepping long and low, veering his head from side to side as though he was a Canada goose entering a spread of decoys.

Boom!

With the picture of his swaying beard just entering my brain, the shotgun's recoil sent me backward. Ross pounced from the brush and kept the bird from flopping while I picked myself up and let out a triumphant whoop.

We had just begun to admire the gobbler when Ross reached down, fanned the bird's beard across his hand and gave me a dumfounded stare.

"I don't believe it," he said.

It didn't take long for my untrained eye to discover the bird was a mature gobbler, but I wondered silently if he wasn't some kind of freak. I mean, what was the deal with all those strands of hair protruding from his sleek breast?

"He's got five beards!" Ross said.

I couldn't help but have fun with the moment.

"Uh, is that like a good one, or something?" I asked.

Ross' expression said it all.

"You lucky stiff."

Land of Cotton and Rain

My hunt originated soon after my associate editor position with *Deer & Deer Hunting* was expanded to include working with its sister publication, *Turkey & Turkey Hunting*.

I was certainly out of my element, but this turkey hunt reconfirmed an adage I use in the deer woods: Patience and perseverance don't usually go unrewarded. Besides, I was hunting with some of the best hunters and callers in the nation.

The hunt was hosted by Jerry Peterson and Gary Sefton of Woods Wise Products and Winchester's Kevin Howard and Mike Jordan. They picked Alabama's White Oak Plantation because, as Sefton said when we arrived, "It don't get much better than this."

Although I had to absorb decades worth of turkey knowledge in a few days, I found it more difficult to deal with the weather. Incessant rain soaked our spirits the first two days by shutting off gobbling.

I was told not to fret, because lovesick gobblers wouldn't let a little water get in the way of their mission. Sefton told me the key to hunting turkeys in the rain is to adopt an aggressive attitude.

"The first thing you have to do is get the blood running through his veins," Sefton said. "Then, you can work him just like you would on a sunny day. The hard part is getting the gobblers to respond. You need something out of the ordinary."

Another dose of good advice came from White Oak owner Bo Pitman.

"There have been times when I've set up on a bird in the morning and haven't left that one tree until dark," he said. "Every situation is different, but the easiest way to kill a gobbler in the rain is to figure out his routine and then wait him out."

Searching for Food

To figure out the patterns of those rainy-day gobblers, we went straight for the food sources.

On Day 3 of the hunt, Pitman and I covered several miles of his 20,000-acre operation in search of active gobblers. We trudged through swamps and dense hardwoods to reach pastures, pine forests and crop fields, but we came up empty.

Pitman said it's unusual to cover so much land in search of an active gobbler. In fact, he said it's common to find at least two birds per square mile.

"Of course, there are no 'for-sures' in turkey hunting," he said.

For us to succeed in the rain, Pitman said, we would have to concentrate on fields of clover, wheat and hay. These open areas allowed birds to feed while paying attention to danger.

In fact, Pitman said grass fields are good bets for finding spring turkeys in all weather. In the South, grass fields offer plenty of food such as seeds and insects. In wet weather, turkeys especially love these fields because rain slows down crickets and grasshoppers, making them easier to catch.

"Hardwoods are ideal, but turkeys do love a grass we call deertongue," Pitman said. "They also love panic grass."

Mistakes and New Tactics

As much as I tried to focus on the advice the veterans were giving me, I still managed to make a classic mistake: moving too much.

I quickly learned I couldn't get away with the subtle movements of my head, hands and feet I've gotten away with for years in deer stands.

"You mean I can't do that?" I said to one of my guides when I slowly turned my wrist to check the time. He didn't answer. The putts from a retreating hen provided my answer.

In fact, too much body movement even dooms seasoned hunters who come to Alabama for the first time, Pitman said.

"Most people don't realize how much they move even when they think they're holding still," he said.

Sefton agreed.

"Alabama turkeys are about as stressed as any (in the United States). They're even more wary than northern birds, probably because they're used to being stirred up 12 months out of the year. If it's not hunters, it's by other predators."

However, Sefton added that the rainy weather we hunted in is more forgiving than ideal conditions.

"You can really get away with a lot more in this type of weather," he said. "The mistakes people make when it's not raining are usually the things I do when it is raining."

For example, Sefton said he calls louder and more often when it's raining, and he isn't afraid to pick up and move in an attempt to find a receptive gobbler.

"I try to force things," Sefton said. "You usually can't do that when the weather is nice."

Back to the Hunt

By the end of Day 4, I was feeling fortunate. I had not only killed the gobbler of a lifetime, I had watched the veteran hunters team with the White Oak guides to beat the rain and kill eight longbeards. Among that group was outdoor writer John Trout, who bagged a dandy gobbler that sported 1¼-inch spurs and a 9-inch beard.

Of course, my instant success gave me reason to stay motivated. I guess my actions said it all as we assembled in the dining hall before our last morning of hunting. Robert Pitman noticed I was fidgeting.

"You're hooked!" Pitman exclaimed. "We got you!"

Floating from enthusiasm, I headed to the woods with Bo Pitman and Howard in an attempt to kill my second bird.

Putting the Pieces Together

The crash course in turkey hunting started making sense when I watched Pitman analyze the damp hardwoods as we set up on an oak ridge. Pitman positioned Howard so he could watch an open draw, and had me pointing south, facing the ridge's crown.

Analyzing the surroundings at daylight, Pitman decided the aggressive approach was necessary. He quietly left his position to tell me that Howard had heard a distant gobble.

"Let's go get 'em," he said. Soon, we were heading toward the hot gobbler.

With Howard and me doing our best to avoid prickly snares and low-hanging branches, Pitman led us on a near dash through a swamp. He then stopped on a ridge and worked his slate call. The gobbler responded. Pitman knew where to go — to an open area.

Ten minutes and several hundred yards later later, Pitman stopped near a grassy area near an electric right-of-way. He let out another series of yelps, and the bird gobbled again. The tom was working an open area not too far from a road.

It was set-up time. Howard ducked next to a fallen log near a tree, while I scurried behind Pitman and set up on top of the hill in a tree line.

Pitman struck his slate once more, and then put it away.

Desperately wanting female companionship, the bird gobbled. And gobbled. And gobbled. When he realized his hen wasn't getting closer, he decided to turn and come toward us.

When the bird crested a rise 12 yards to my left, he was met with a load of No. 6 shot. The 19-pound gobbler sported a 10-inch beard and 1-inch spurs.

Conclusion

This first turkey hunting trip taught me more about America's most adaptable game bird than I could have hoped to learn in years of self study. Above all, I learned that good woodsmanship skills are as important — if not more — in turkey hunting as they are in deer hunting.

Sure, I'll probably never get a crack at another 5-bearder, but I will forever see him strutting into view when I'm sitting patiently in the woods.

Turkey hunting.

Robert Pitman was right. I'm hooked.

— Daniel Schmidt, editor of Deer & Deer Hunting *magazine, has continued his turkey hunting passion and killed many more gobblers.*

CHAPTER 3

The Tin Box

As I recall my turkey hunting career, it's odd how little things, such as my dad's old Phillips Tablets box, stick in my mind. That little silver container was the answer to many problems he encountered in the spring woods.

■ RON JOLLY

I never knew where he got the idea. I only knew that an old Phillips Tablets box held the "secret" call. My dad, Junior, carefully reworked it each night. He was very particular about who saw or heard the call, because it was the answer to many problems he encountered in the spring turkey woods.

Colors of Yesteryear

In those days, my dad's turkey hunting attire consisted of a khaki shirt, blue jeans, a dull-colored cap and rubber boots. There were no camo, facemasks or gloves.

Dad carried the box in his shirt pocket. Through the years, the paint and lettering had faded away, leaving the box completely silver. Inside the container, Dad's mouth call was carefully wrapped in toilet tissue. The box also contained materials to repair the call, which my dad did frequently. Often, he made a series of just three yelps. Each note sounded like music to my ears, but after calling, Dad often dismantled and reassembled the call on the spot.

Many times, I was afraid a gobbler would catch Dad as he made his repairs. However, I cannot remember that happening.

The box carried an assortment of turkey call materials that, by today's standards, were crude. It held a single-edged razor blade, white medical tape cut to fit the call's crude frames and pieces of a Trojan condom — unlubricated, of course.

The call consisted of two identical aluminum pieces. The condom formed the reed, and tape held everything together. How Dad knew how much tension to place on the reed remains a mystery. However, each time he put the call together, it sounded the same.

One April morning, Dad led me to a roosted gobbler and set up behind a large pecan log. The old Model 12 Winchester rested across the log, pointing in the general direction of the bird.

That morning loomed ominous with heavy thunder and lightning to the west. I asked Dad if we could come back after the storm passed, but he wouldn't have it.

"That gobbler isn't too good to sit in the rain, so why should we be?" he replied.

As daylight approached, so did the storm. To rush the issue, Dad did something I rarely saw him do: He called to the gobbler while it was still roosted.

Dad's three soft yelps were answered by a thundering gobble. For the next two hours, the longbeard gobbled repeatedly at the approaching spring storm. Through it all, Dad never called.

The morning seemed to forget sunrise and daylight. The approaching storm provided a hint of dawn when lightning seared across the sky and lit the hardwood forest. The sound of the thunder was so loud it hurt my ears, but the gobbler answered it every time.

Dad was at ease, but I was ready to go home

'That's When We'll Get Him'

I cannot forget how relaxed Dad seemed for the two hours the storm raged. I still get chills when I recall how the storm engulfed us and our quarry.

What began as a setup on the dry forest floor soon turned into a miserable ordeal for a 10-year-old boy. Soon, Dad and I lay on our bellies behind the pecan log in 8 inches of fresh, cold rainwater.

Finally, the storm began to let up. Dad took his call from the box and began tearing it apart. The routine was always the same.

Dad carefully placed the two aluminum halves on his knee in horseshoe-to-horseshoe fashion. He then took the tape in his left hand and cradled it in his palm. Then, he placed the two halves of the frame on the tape. When everything was in place, he carefully placed the piece of condom over half the frame with his right hand. With the thumb and forefinger of his right hand, Dad gently stretched the rubber and held it in place. Then, he flipped the top half of the frame atop of the reed with the middle finger of his left hand. When the halves were aligned, Dad applied pressure to the call with his finger to hold tension on the reed. He then pressed the excess tape around the frame together to hold the call in place.

That sounds complicated, but Dad could rebuild the call in less than two minutes. Of course, the tape only lasted briefly in his mouth before it became wet and let the reed lose tension.

On that stormy April morning, I watched as Dad prepared the call. When it was ready, he carefully returned it to the box, put it in his shirt pocket and settled behind the log.

The turkey hadn't gobbled since the rain started more than an hour earlier. However, the downpour was easing, and the thunder had moved to the east. I was ready to leave, because every inch of my body was wet, and I was cold to the bone.

Finally, Dad turned toward me.

"When the rain stops, that old gobbler will shake the rain off his back and fly down," he said. "That's when we'll get him."

The Box Yields Another

Thirty minutes later, the rain had stopped. I was shaking uncontrollably from the cold.

Suddenly, however, a gobble boomed. The longbeard was finally on the ground.

Dad took the box from his pocket, removed the call and placed it in his mouth. Three yelps yielded another gobble. He then took the call from his mouth and returned it to the box.

Thirty minutes later, the bird appeared. I still remember the sight of that old tom as he walked in front of the fallen pecan log. The rain had stopped more than an hour before, but the gobbler still looked like a drowned rat. When the bird was 25 yards away, the old Model 12 ended the ordeal for me — and the turkey.

The sight of that longbeard carefully walking to us will never leave my memory. I can still see his tail bob as he waded through the 8-inch deep pools, and he seemed to know that he shouldn't step farther into the standing water. When the load of No. 6 shot took him down, the turkey's flopping churned the water to a chocolate brown. His feathers seemed to melt against his body.

Dad proudly grabbed the gobbler by the feet and tossed him across his shoulder. It was the ugliest turkey I had seen, but to Dad, he was a special prize. He had outwitted another tom with the secret call.

The elements didn't hamper his turkey hunt, and they didn't prevent him from teaching his son another lesson.

Conclusion

As I recall my turkey hunting career, it's odd how little things, such as that old Phillips Tablets box, stick in my mind. I believe those little things make turkey hunting so special.

It must be the same for all who know and hunt this grand bird.

— Longtime Turkey & Turkey Hunting *contributor Ron Jolly has hunted and filmed turkeys across the country.*

CHAPTER 4

The Miracle of Spring

A day in the spring woods heals my being, letting me set aside worries and concerns until another day. Who doesn't need such an opportunity?

■ ROGER B. HOOK

Spring is a time for rebirth. It's when the cold days of winter give way to the chill of longer, warmer promises. Birds sing lustily. The sun shines brighter and again invites plants to spring from dormancy. Redbuds bloom, soon to be followed by the white blossoms of dogwoods. Nature nods its approval.

The arrival of spring reminds all life that beyond the cold, dark nights of winter, there's new hope. Because life is difficult, most of us need spring. It's a welcome sight.

The High Stress Lifestyle

In the 1950s and early 1960s, Americans were told that by the late 1980s and certainly the 1990s, we would be working about three to four days per week, and would have more leisure time than we would know what to do with. However, in modern society, many families need more than one income to pay their bills, and people work more hours than workers a few years ago.

Most Americans — men and women — are stressed to the limit. The demands of our lifestyle can be costly. At the turn of this century, the leading causes of death stemmed from poor nutrition and lack of medical knowledge and attention. Nowadays, stress-induced illnesses lead the way — too often to an early grave.

More than ever, people must recharge their batteries. They need outlets and ways to enjoy life. We have been taught there's only one pace in life — all out. Anything less is unacceptable. Unfortunately, we have bought this idea.

I look forward to spring because I take time from my routine to enjoy turkey hunting. Nothing clears cobwebs from my mind or rejuvenates my spirit more than entering the spring woods.

Spring turkey hunting involves more than killing gobblers, although I won't apologize for killing some each spring. For me, turkey hunting adds balance to life. A day in the spring woods heals my being, letting me set aside worries and concerns until another day. Who doesn't need such an opportunity?

Share the Sport

On a ridgetop several years ago, I shared turkey hunting's appeal with my son, Brian. That morning, when Brian was 12, he called to his first turkey. The smile that spread across his face when the gobbler responded is etched forever in my memory. Life's pressures seemed removed from what we shared that morning, and mention of that hunt still redirects my thoughts and creates peace during tumultuous times.

Each year, I share the spring woods with someone new. Those hunts have developed friendships and strengthened relationships. I've become fonder of nature's things, which are meant to be shared.

Last spring, I spent three rainy days in southern Texas trying to lure a Rio for my wife, Deloris. I had built her up for the hunt.

"You will hear turkeys gobbling in every direction," I said.

However, it wasn't meant to be. Rain dampens Rios' amorous desires. At the end of Deloris' first hunt, I was more disappointed than her. I badly wanted to see the excitement on her face as she watched her first turkey strut into view.

A week after we returned from Texas, we hunted our family farm. I felt Deloris' heartbeat quicken and her muscles tense as two Easterns approached during a cool, windy spring morning. I looked down the gun barrel when she pulled the trigger. The shot was high and left of the gobbler's head. The turkey was the first living thing she'd shot at. Deloris' time on the sporting clays range bailed her out, though, because she dumped the gobbler with a perfect wingshot.

At one time, gobblers were scarce. However, the days of hunting a season without working a turkey have passed,

Brian Lovett

thanks to game management. During those difficult days, hunters were understandably reluctant to share hunts or information about a gobbler's whereabouts. Nowadays, only selfish hunters guard their strategies and refuse to take friends along.

The thrill of watching a tom pitch from his roost to the forest floor, blow up in full strut, and cautiously drum and strut to calling occupies the mind. There's no room for concern about unpaid bills, the stock market or rain for the crops. The sights and sounds of that moment are enough.

Experienced spring hunters find added fulfillment by introducing novices to such wonders. How often have we repeated the cliche, "There's nothing like it."? It's unconscionable to hoard the miracle of spring.

Lessons for Life

Spring turkey hunting has taught me the importance of patience. I'm not talking about the patience required for a successful hunt, but the patience you must have with people. Every day, someone will test your patience, just like an old gobbler that refuses to come in. Perhaps it will happen when you're driving down the highway, standing in line at the grocery store or waiting on medical tests for a loved one. Patience is good.

The sights and sounds of spring engulf the soul. Much of life robs us of pieces of our ourselves. Who hasn't been overlooked for a job promotion? Who has avoided being treated unfairly? Who has escaped the impact of divorce or death? Grief, although difficult, is part of life.

We need the miracle of spring. We need something that immerses us in nature so we can walk away bone-tired yet emotionally recharged. The fabric of life is thin. Miracle mornings lend texture.

I remember a late-spring morning when I walked into the woods emotionally spent. The previous days had been long, tiring and trying. Before first light, a tom gobbled. I knew him, because he had beaten me several days earlier.

The Rejuvenation

I could smell spring's sweet fragrance as I set up. I almost forgot about the turkey call in my mouth as I listened to a whippoorwill's song. There was a hunter on the next ridge, and I knew he could hear the gobbler. For some reason, though, he stayed on his ridge, almost as if he knew I needed a miracle.

Dawn turned to day, and crows cawed at a red-tailed hawk searching for food. The more the crows shouted, the more my gobbler carried on. The experience was greater than I deserved. I believed I was where I belonged.

Brian Lovett

The gobbler cooperated. He was without hens that morning and came to my calling. His gobbles shook the earth as he neared, and he appeared ghostlike 30 yards away. My shotgun was locked on his blood-red wattles, and the moment seemed in harmony with nature — even when a coyote charged in without warning and ran the gobbler off. I could only laugh. It felt good. I sat there and soaked up the sun's warmth. The day's demanding tasks awaited me when I returned home, but my spirit was renewed.

A long walk in the spring woods, listening to the crunch of leaves, can be therapeutic. Everyone must discover therapy: experiences that breathe life into us, and ways that let us discover our uniqueness. Spring turkey hunting, beyond the satisfaction of killing a bird, can replace a therapist's couch or help us avoid it.

Much of life is incongruent. People of all ages, especially teen-agers, try to make sense of everything. Many have never experienced nature. They only know what it's like to be surrounded by concrete high-rise buildings and the temptation of drugs.

They need someone to show them the beauty of nature. The screech of a tree frog and the hoot of a barred owl are foreign to them, and they are lesser for it. Youngsters are well-schooled in computers and electronic games, but most

have never seen a wild turkey or heard one gobble. Have we prepared them for the next century?

Looking Forward

Turkey hunting also gives us something to look forward to. Beyond dreams of future hunts, we must plan and complete many tasks. Some hunters practice calling, shuffle their spring schedules, find new places to hunt, or sort through reading materials.

I look forward to February, when turkey calling contests begin and the National Wild Turkey Federation holds its annual convention. These events let me add to my collection of toys. Just as I enjoy watching my 15-month-old grandson dump his toys on the floor and play with them, I enjoy acquiring more turkey toys and playing with them.

The spare bedroom in our home has a large dresser that's off limits to everyone but me. It holds my spring toys. One drawer contains my box calls, and another holds my friction calls. A small narrow drawer is filled with suction calls and strikers for friction calls. Another drawer holds my diaphragm calls, and several drawers contain my camouflage. I cherish these toys. I bought many, but some were gifts. I have a box call signed by Preston Pittman and a friction call given to me by Mike Battey, who is to friction calls what M.L. Lynch is to box calls. Some of my favorites include prototype calls manufacturers gave me a year or more before they hit the market.

Conclusion

Spring turkey hunting is essential. Although I enjoy the offseason, recalling hunts and playing with my toys, the true escape and diversion occurs during spring. My heart quickens when a gobbler drums and struts. The miracle of spring, with its sights, sounds and smells, captivates me. I need it.

If you need to add fun to your life, go to the spring woods. Absorb everything. Let them transform you. Smell the aroma, and listen to the sounds. Watch the foliage spring to life. Challenge a boss gobbler, and learn his ways. Exercise your mind, body and spirit. Set aside the worries and brokenness everyone experiences.

Perhaps spring will heal you. Maybe you will experience a miracle, as I do every spring.

— Roger Hook, a Methodist minister and turkey calling expert, is a longtime contributor to Turkey & Turkey Hunting.

Brian Lovett

CHAPTER 5

The Old Account

You never know why turkey hunting suddenly switches from joyful and simple to harrowing and difficult. It just does.

■ *BRIAN LOVETT*

Rise now, turkey hunter. Reflect on your fate and receive your sentence. Come on, get up; get off your belly and out of the mud. Let the cold rain dribble down the back of your cap, into your collar and, eventually, down your back.

Wipe the grime off your still-smoking shotgun, and kick the dirt clods from your boots. Spit out your mouth call, curse at your now-soaked striker and wonder aloud to no one how you could have screwed up something so wonderful.

Whispered Tales of Woe

You've just missed a gobbler, of course, so you're down.

Ah, but it wasn't any old gobbler. You'd struck the big boy at midmorning and worked him skillfully to within 60 yards — right to a hen that intercepted him. You'd belly-crawled through wet woods to the edge of a corn-stubble field, peering out through the haze and increasing downpour to spot the top of his fan just over the crest.

Patiently and carefully, you'd clucked and purred the hen to within 40 yards as the gobbler hung just out of range behind her. And when he'd finally decided to leave the field, you'd clucked sharply and calmly squeezed the trigger,

Brian Lovett

179

whizzing a swarm of No. 6 shot past his head and sending him flying across the ravine to parts unknown.

Game over. Hunt finished. Day done. The turkey wins by unanimous decision. And you! You can waddle back to your truck, straining your drenched boots with each step to kick yourself in your soggy rear end.

Along the way, you'll envision the bewildered looks from friends and co-workers. Soon, the voices start to whisper.

"No turkey?"

"What happened?"

"You did what?"

"Why, so-and-so just went and sat in the woods for 10 minutes this afternoon and killed one."

Sure, there's nothing to it; nothing at all. And you'll tell 'em that — maybe in a few months, when you believe it again.

The Pinnacle

It hasn't always been this way. No, there have been sunny days when turkeys acted like turkeys, and your planning, maneuvering, calling and shooting had been clinic-in-the-woods perfect. Those bygone hunts seemed distant and hazy, but you remembered.

There had been other days, too; "hallelujah mornings" when fortune and fate met at your setups, sending suicidal gobblers sailing from their roosts and sprinting to the gun. There had been late-in-the-day Hail Marys when your stealth and skill let you score miraculous last-minute gobblers from otherwise woeful hunts. There had been hellacious gobbles that cut off your cutting, followed by a quick sit-down and an approaching softball head. And there had been those shining arrivals at lodges and camps, where fellow hunters praised your success and hailed your acumen.

But such moments don't last. Never do.

No, you might ride a streak for a few days, maybe a week or — once every 10 years or so — a season. But things change.

It's subtle at first. A rainy day ends a streak of good gobbling weather. A tough shot breaks a streak of dead-on kills. An aggressive move goes one step too far, spooking a bird instead of gaining ground on him.

And then, my friend, the ride has reached the zenith. You've gone up like a shot, paused at the peak to appreciate the view and sensed a slight drop. Soon, you're barreling toward the ground in a free-fall. Funny, but the trip down seems longer than the ascent.

Birds won't gobble. Your calling stinks. You commit blunder after blunder in the woods. And as your pals pile up spurs, beards and stories, you silently stew and listen again for the whispers behind your camouflaged back.

"What's he doing wrong?"

"He's not being patient enough."

"He should know better."

There must be a bottom to the fall. There has to be. Sure, things will turn around. But when?

You'll never know. And you'll never know why the fun ride suddenly turns scary. It just does.

After enough highs and lows in the spring woods, you realize better than anyone that turkey hunting is just a roller-coaster ride in the dark.

Go Forth

So like you heard before, turkey hunter, get off your belly and out of the mud. Rise, and hear the tale of your sins. But take heart. Like the gospel song says, that old account was wiped clean long ago.

Go forth. You will eventually return to that time and place where things are "right." You might find it at the next place you call, or it might elude you till tomorrow, next week — or next season. But you will find it.

Always have, always will.

Stumble forward — on nothing but faith, if you must — not knowing when, where or how it will finally happen.

Just know.

— Brian Lovett served as editor of Turkey & Turkey Hunting *from August 1995 through January 2002. Currently, he is the editor of* Bass Pro Shops' Outdoor World *magazine.*

Brian Lovett

CHAPTER 6

Turkey Camp

What brings us back to turkey hunting camp year after year? The attraction is difficult to describe, but it's best summed up in my mind by images of people, places and hunts that, Lord willing, I will carry until I die.

■ CHIP GROSS

A nonhunting friend recently said he once visited a turkey camp, and that all the hunters talked about — from morning till night — was turkeys and turkey hunting.

"Don't you guys ever talk about anything else at turkey camp?" he said. "Don't you have families, jobs or whatever to discuss?"

I had to admit that he was probably right.

Yes, we have families and love them. Some of us even love our jobs. But what he didn't understand is that for a fleeting few weeks of spring each year, we are children again — children with no cares other than chasing gobblers, with few thoughts of our everyday world.

My friend's question also made me think about what pulls us back to turkey hunting camp every year. The attraction is difficult to describe, but it's best summed up in my mind by images of people, places and hunts that, Lord willing, I will carry until I die.

Brian Lovett

Camouflaged shotguns leaning in corners.

Wet clothes hung over a warm wood stove to dry.

Alarm clocks sounding in unison at 4 a.m.

Topographic maps studied every night at the kitchen table, their curled corners held down by boxes of shotgun shells.

Hearty meals served on mismatched plates, cups and silverware.

An empty magnum hull beside a fresh turkey beard.

Fanned turkey tails pinned on cardboard.

Hunting regulations on dresser tops.

Muddy boots on the back porch, and muddy vehicles parked outside.

Box calls sitting tuned, chalked and ready.

Snapshots of gobblers taped to the kitchen walls.

The same old dog-eared outdoors magazines in the bathroom year after year.

An occasional stray breast feather wafting to the floor.

Rumpled sleeping bags on sagging mattresses.

Mist rising off the hills as you look out the kitchen window after a shower.

An afternoon napper snoring from the bedroom.

A handful of 3-inch shells on an end table.

Hunting stories, old and new, told while sitting on the back porch.

Sons learning to become men.

Daughters learning you can enjoy hunting and still be ladies.

Why do we love it? What is it that attracts us to turkey camp? Maybe Spanish philosopher Jose Ortega y Gasset said it best in his classic book Meditations on Hunting:

"This is the reason men hunt. When you are fed up with the troublesome present, with being 'very 20th century,' you take your gun ... go out to the mountain and, without further ado, give yourself ... pleasure during a few hours or a few days ... "

It's not just the opportunity to hear and hunt a gobbler that brings us back to turkey camp, because many of us could do that closer to home. No, turkey camp is much more than that. It's a combination of camaraderie, stories, ribbing and respect that makes us return. It's old friends, new friends and a chance — if only for a while — to be children again.

— *Chip Gross is a turkey hunter and free-lance writer from Ohio.*

Brian Lovett

Brian Lovett

Brian Lovett

CHAPTER 7

The Wet Rat II

The old gobbler gave me the chance to hunt him every morning on the farm — something I worried I would not be able to do in years to come.

■ MICHAEL HANBACK

I paused to the side of the power line, not wanting to cross the opening in case the gobbler was roosted in the big pines on the opposite edge. It was one of those damp, bone-chilling mornings when daylight lags and covers your movements, but I was still leery of bumping the turkey. I sat on a wet log and waited.

Rain or shine, every spring morning is a new beginning. As you sit and wait for the woods to turn from black to gray to "gobbling light," you can't help but think about your job, your money, your children — all the things going on in your hectic life.

That dreary day, I pondered something else: the fate of the James farm. I had always had bigger and better places to hunt, but this was my secret spot. Here, many years ago, I had killed my first buck, a fat spike, and felt its hot blood on my hands. Here I had called in and shot my first long-bearded turkey on my own, without my dad's help. Here I had come so many times after school and on weekends, accomplishing things I never thought I could.

Unstoppable Change

I sat, shivering and worried. The recent years had brought staggering change to this part of Virginia. People had flocked en masse from the big city to enjoy our country life. The tentacles of suburbia — the housing developments, shopping centers and new roads — had sprawled and crawled throughout our once-quiet and peaceful community. A decade ago I knew everybody in town. Now, I hardly recognized a soul. How had it happened so fast, changing the land and our way of life seemingly overnight?

For years, the James farm had been spared the spade, but now the squeeze was on. One spring not long ago, a subdivision popped up on the western edge of the property. That fall, I sat in a deer stand and listened as dozers ripped new roads into the woods from the east and south. The neighboring landowners were selling lots and turning a quick buck. It was only a matter of time until old man James got rid of his cattle and sold out to a developer. And who was I to blame him? He'd make millions.

I remember listening from that very spot on April mornings years ago. The call of the whippoorwill and the barred owl, the chatter of jays at first light, the mooing of cows in the nearby pasture, the sweet sounds of the rural South. Now, dogs barked, house lights flickered through the trees, and SUVs roared as commuters zoomed off for the city while I sat hoping and praying that the turkey would ...

"Gaaaarrrrobbbble!"

The Wet Rat

There, in the pines across the power line — the Wet Rat!

I had named the turkey the first time I had met him, a week earlier on a drizzly morning like this. After slipping across the power line in the gloom, I had sat beneath an enormous oak that had grown on the farm since the days when our native son, Stonewall Jackson, had chased the Yankees out of this part of Virginia. The oak sat on a ridge where you could hear a turkey a long way while envisioning gray and blue soldiers clashing fiercely for our soil in the misty pre-dawn. The old oak was my favorite listening post for many reasons.

That morning the previous week, the turkey had gobbled on his own in a pine tree 50 yards away! I had flinched, peeked up and saw his odd silhouette etched in the pewter sky. The tom's feathers were soaked and matted after a long night of sleeping in the rain, which made his glimmering white head look enormous. The bird's tailfeathers were soggy, and his beard was twisted together like a strand of licorice.

"You look like a wet rat," I had thought before wondering just what the heck to do with the turkey roosted so close.

It would have been smart to do, well, nothing. I could have waited 20 minutes or so for the bird to pitch down. If he landed on my side of the pine tree, I could have inched up my shotgun and whacked him. But what fun would that have been? I had eked out a tiny yelp on a diaphragm.

"Gaaarrrobble!"

I'd jumped a foot when the Rat roared, but somehow he didn't see me. The turkey hung on his limb for half an hour, gobbling, and I was struck with some strange thoughts.

Surely, all the commuters leaving for work could hear the Rat's raucous melody. Then again, maybe not. Those were city folk, and their ears weren't tuned to calls of the wild. Could they envision a camouflaged country boy sitting in the dreary woods less than a mile away, smiling and shivering every time the turkey bellowed? I doubt if those groggy-eyed people knew or gave a damn what was happening in the nearby woods as they rushed off to the office.

Finale

Suddenly, the Wet Rat had flexed his wings and sailed away down the power line. I vowed to return and hunt him the rest of the season. The soggy turkey had become an odd symbol of the changing times in my Virginia.

I hunted the Rat the next six mornings and patterned his movements. After flying from his roost, he would swing to the west and cut within 100 yards of the new homes. I found his tracks in a mud road that had been carved into a building lot to the north. From there, the turkey would strut back toward the section of power line that cut through the James place.

When the turkey gobbled the seventh morning, I circled far below him, crossed the power line, slipped within 300 yards of his roost and sat down. Normally I like to sneak much closer to a tom, but I had already tried several tight positions on the Rat, including the ridiculously close setup the first morning. The turkey had no hens, and he gobbled his fool head off. However, when he hit the ground, he would shun my calls and begin his strut march.

The old turkey was just being an old turkey, but to me he was showing fierce independence. I admired that. The Rat gave me the chance to hunt him every morning on the farm, something I worried I would not be able to do in years to come.

From my setup, I could barely hear the gobbler ringing the damp, heavy air. When he shut up, I knew he was on the ground and on the move. I gave him 30 minutes to make his rounds. During that time more houselights flickered on through the trees, more cars popped gravel in driveways and sped away, more dogs barked and some guy took out his garbage, capping the aluminum trash can with a booming clatter. Once things settled down a bit, I yelped on a box.

"Gaaarrobble!"

The turkey was right where I expected him to be, and I sensed he was coming.

The Rat popped up in the foliage, his huge head glimmering above his matted feathers. His scraggly beard was a good 10 inches long, but no thicker than a black crayon. The turkey exploded into strut, and his rumpled tail feathers were beautiful in an ugly way. The Rat hadn't been dry during the week-long rainy spell, and he showed it.

My 12-gauge boomed for the last time on the farm.

I slung the turkey over my shoulder. His breast was hot and heavy on my back, and the poke of his spurs felt wonderful in my hands. The sun burned through the clouds and shone silver in the woods. Birds trilled and crows cawed. A cow mooed out in the pasture. Down the power line, a Cat fired up, rumbling and coughing black smoke. Carpenters hammered away on another new house to the west. It seemed like a weird dream as I walked away from the farm for the last time.

Keep Smiling ...
and Remembering

In the 21st century, the sport of hunting faces all sorts of challenges. To me, no threat is greater than the loss of small farms and woodlands across the country; those hallowed places where for years boys have gone to roam, hunt and grow from boys to men.

That saddens me, but what can you do about progress? I just roll with the punches and smile every time I ride by what is left of the old James place, remembering all the good times and especially the Wet Rat.

— *Michael Hanback, a contributing editor for* Turkey & Turkey Hunting, *is one of the country's best-known turkey and big-game hunting writers.*

CHAPTER 8

And Your Land Espoused

I guess my boots probably still carry some mud from those spots. Whether I'd killed a turkey in all those places — I hadn't — mattered little. Like someone once said, being there was the thing.

■ BRIAN LOVETT

As I stepped from the oaks onto a narrow ledge, a stiff spring wind caught my cap, sending it sailing to the ground.

I stooped to retrieve my hat and paused for a moment. Below, a steep, rocky incline led to a jungle of multiflora rose and berry bushes. Above, an oak-covered flat angled to meet a rocky peak. All around, the green peaks and valleys of south-central Wisconsin's Baraboo Bluffs rose and fell.

This was distant yet familiar stuff. I'd never tromped this ridge or cast yelps into the hollow, but the earth and sky in this tiny corner of the world were old pals.

I'd grown up a few miles down the interstate. I had shot my first deer one sunny November day about a mile over the oak-studded hill to my right. One May morning, I'd caught my first walleyes and white bass in the surging river to the east. During subsequent autumns, I'd shot squirrels

191

and rabbits in endless woods and thickets atop the bluffs, and I'd spent steamy June afternoons lifting suckers and creek chubs from the tiny creek that carved out the valley floor.

There were no turkeys then, of course. They hadn't arrived — courtesy of trap-and-transplant — till after I'd left the area for college. I'd never thrilled at a spring gobble during those early fishing trips, nor watched from a deer stand as a fall flock of hens and poults drifted through a hardwood ravine.

Those adventures had begun years later and a lifetime away.

Along the Way

I'd taken those early ridge-country lessons with me, of course. They'd been with me fresh out of school, as I'd bumbled and stumbled along distant bluffs during my first turkey hunt. And they'd remained four springs later, when — still bumbling and stumbling — I killed my first gobbler.

A few more lucky hunts followed, fanning the turkey flames high. Not long afterward, my career followed the new passion, and the world opened wide.

The scenes that played out the next several years remain fresh and bright. I can still smell the fresh, moist Alabama river bottom from my initial Dixie hunt, and I still feel the crisp oak leaves crunching under my boots on that first Missouri ridge. Sometimes, I envision the massive white oaks that crown Land Between the Lakes in Kentucky, or see curlews swirling over a deep, cypress-laden Florida swamp.

The jolting shock and fear I'd felt after nearly stepping on a Texas rattler has never left me. And as my legs burned during walks up myriad hills, I think back to my "death marches" in the rocky Sierra Madre Occidental range of Sonora, Mexico.

Sometimes, my mind's eye drifts to the waving grass prairies of South Dakota; the wide, cottonwood-dotted vistas of Nebraska's Sandhills; or the seemingly endless green peaks of Virginia and West Virginia.

When all is quiet, I hear rooster pheasants salute the dawn in the open farmland of Iowa and Kansas, the heavy March rain begin tapping the pines in the Low Country of South Carolina, or the morning's first cardinals kick off the day high atop deep forest hills in Arkansas or New York.

I guess my boots probably still carry some mud from those spots. Whether I'd killed a turkey in all those places — I hadn't — mattered little. Like someone once said, being there was the thing.

Brian Lovett

Splinters of the Mind's Eye

By nature, turkey hunting is fickle. Its constant peaks and valleys leave you hanging your head or believing your own boasts.

But the stage remains.

At the risk of slapping myself on the back too hard, I think I realized that early. I've tried to appreciate every piece of ground on which I've ever chased a gobbler. No matter whether gobbling was deafening or nonexistent, there were still oak buds straining for precious sunlight, and spring peepers chiming at dawn and dusk. And when you could do nothing right — or, now and then, wrong — in the woods, spring still churned along, renewing life and perpetuating a cycle that had been repeated for eons.

Maybe it was the contrasts that amazed me. Turkeys — north, south, east or west — are turkeys. Sure, some might have had physiological differences from their subspecies cousins miles away, but they are still turkeys. But how the scenes varied.

You might run the same series of yelps on the same friction call and receive the same response day after day. Yet one gobble might come from the cover of a deep Dixie river bottom, but others from the far end of a massive Texas cattle pasture or a high prairie break along an ancient Midwestern river. And ill-advised movement would still spook any gobbler, whether he lived in a long creek bottom in southeastern Kansas, a foggy beech ridge near the Finger Lakes of New York, or a Florida cypress swamp that might have seen Spanish visitors centuries ago.

Better, I learned that if you sat against those trees, crawled through that grass or traversed those winding paths, you assuredly carry a small piece of them with you — a connection that forever binds you with earth, sky, flora and fauna of that place and time. Years might fade those recollections somewhat, but memories renew easily with the whiff of a familiar flower or the cry of a distant bird — even if the fragments of thought are buried deep.

Renewing the Bond

Which brought me back to that ridge.

I walked along it that day, straining through popples just a few years old and slipping through oaks that had been there since before I knew the area existed.

I was serious about calling and hunting turkeys, but I don't mind telling you that none died that day. In fact, none came close to dying.

When I stowed my vest and met up with a friend, we shook our heads and cursed our misfortune. Maybe it would improve the next day, he wondered aloud.

Maybe. Maybe not.

Either way, the invitation for another reunion and nostalgia trip with that rich ground was too much to pass up.

And later, as I pulled my truck onto the highway for the long drive home, I hoped the dirt from that high ridge would never fall from my boots.

— Brian Lovett served as editor of Turkey & Turkey Hunting *from August 1995 through January 2002. Currently, he is the editor of* Bass Pro Shops' Outdoor World *magazine.*

CHAPTER 9

In the Footsteps of the Intimidator

Just two months after Dale Earnhardt's death, we stood where he had killed his final turkey. Hearing the details of the hunt from its only witness was a moving experience, even for non-NASCAR fans.

■ *JILL EASTON AND JIM SPENCER*

It looked like dozens of other western Georgia cow pastures, but this Troup County farm held a bit of turkey hunting legend.

It was where Dale Earnhardt, the Man in Black, NASCAR's famous Intimidator, killed his last gobbler. We were there a year later, hunting with the guy who had been with Earnhardt when he pulled the trigger that final time.

Earnhardt, as everyone who hasn't been in a time warp knows, died Feb. 18, 2001, when his car hit the retaining wall during the final lap of the Daytona 500. Just two months later, we stood on a hillside not far east of LaGrange — precisely where Earnhardt had killed that final bird the previous spring. Hearing the details of the hunt from its only witness was a moving experience, even for non-NASCAR fans.

As we searched unsuccessfully for the empty shotgun hull from that final hunt — wouldn't that have been a trophy? — we listened as Glenn Garner, turkey guide, land manager and Realtree videographer, discussed that hunt and the man behind the public image.

Earnhardt liked to do things fast, whether chasing the checkered flag in his Chevrolet Monte Carlo or chasing a turkey in western Georgia.

"He had zero patience for turkey hunting the traditional way," Garner said. "I'd call a few times, a bird would start coming in, and before you knew it, Dale would be gone, crawling after the gobbler. He wouldn't stay put long enough to get a hunt on tape."

"Dale loved being outdoors almost as much as he loved going fast," said Michael Waddell, producer of Realtree Outdoors. "He was a good woodsman, but he was real short on patience. He didn't have a lot of experience hunting turkeys conventionally, so he always liked going with us because we'd let him hunt the way he wanted to. He especially enjoyed hunting with Glenn."

Earnhardt was one of the winningest drivers in racing history. He was naturally competitive, with a passion for hunting almost as strong as his passion for racing. Not many fans know it, but throughout his career, Earnhardt slipped away at every chance to pursue his second passions: hunting and fishing. One of the few times he almost missed a race was the Talladega 500 in April of 2000 — because of that final turkey hunt.

Fateful Hunt

"It was the hardest rain I'd ever hunted in," Garner said, shivering involuntarily in the warm sunshine as he remembered that wet day. "In two minutes, I was wet down to my underwear, but Dale wanted to go anyway."

It wasn't raining only in Troup County that April morning. In Alabama, qualifying laps at Talladega were postponed because of slow-moving thunderstorms. In fact, the bad weather let Earnhardt hunt that morning. However, if the storms passed, qualifying runs would begin when the track was dry. Earnhardt's plane sat waiting at the Columbus, Ga., airport, 30 miles from where Earnhardt and Garner were hunting and almost 150 miles from the track. If the weather cleared, everyone knew there would be a desperate dash to the airport.

"When we got to hunting that morning, every few hours Dale would call his crew at the track on his cell phone," Garner said. "'This is Earnhardt. What's happening?' As long as the rain continued, he could keep hunting."

The trio of Earnhardt, Garner and David Blanton, executive producer for Realtree Outdoors, spent the morning chasing birds and periodically checking the weather at Talladega. Early in the hunt, Earnhardt missed a gobbler because of the rain, and the birds at another of Garner's hotspots refused to play. The hunters then drove to the Troup County property for a final try.

"After a frustrating morning of missed opportunities, we heard some gobbling and spotted four jakes on this hillside while we were standing over there," Garner said, pointing to a knoll across the valley. "Something told me there ought to be some mature birds in the area, so we decided to get closer to the jakes and see what developed."

To get into calling position, the hunters had to cross the valley and sneak through a patch of woods. From there, they had to low-crawl across a wide-open no-man's-land of short grass and mud to a scraggly clump of bushes halfway up the hill. The rain had stopped temporarily, but as they moved, it came down even harder. Because the downpour wasn't good for Blanton's video equipment, he returned to the truck.

Realtree's other videographers haven't let him forget his "wimpy attitude."

Mud Crawl

"We covered the 100 or so yards across the open ground on our hands and knees in the mud and hard-driving rain," Garner said.

"When we got into position, I called a couple of times, and the jakes came running over the crest of the hill so fast they caught me with the decoy in my hand," Garner said, pointing with both arms as he showed the positions of hunters and turkeys that morning. "Behind the jakes came two gobblers, trying to catch up. We hadn't been able to see the older birds before because they were off to our left under the hill, but here they came anyway. Those two big gobblers had death in their eyes, and they were so fixated on the decoy, they didn't even see me holding it."

As the birds approached, Garner stage-whispered to Earnhardt: "You can probably take both of them, Dale. Don't jump up after the first bird goes down." (Georgia lets hunters kill more than one bird per day.)

Earnhardt nodded, flicked the rain out of his eyes and fired. The leading longbeard went down in a soggy heap.

"Paycheck," he whispered, and then swung on the second bird. However, the wet, muddy shotgun jammed, and the turkey escaped. Earnhardt's bird was a good 2-year-old, with a 10 3/4-inch beard and almost 1-inch spurs.

"After taking the gobbler back to the truck and ragging Blanton a little bit, we went to hunt another place," Garner said.

However, their luck had run out. Earnhardt called Talladega again, and his pit boss told him the rain had stopped and they were drying the track.

"We're gonna have to quit, boys," Earnhardt said with regret. "I've got to go drive a race car."

They rushed back to Garner's house, where Earnhardt changed to dry clothes. Then, he and Blanton sped toward the Columbus airport.

"All the way to the airport, Dale was encouraging me to drive faster," Blanton said.

It was a hair-raising trip for the normally sedate-driving Blanton, trying to keep his vehicle on the wet roads winding through the Georgia clay hills.

"Don't worry if you get stopped," Earnhardt said. "I'll take care of it."

They reached the airport without incident, and Earnhardt made it to the track in time to qualify for the race.

That afternoon, after Earnhardt had won Talladega for the second consecutive year, he told reporters he'd almost missed qualifying because of the turkey hunt. Actually, the qualifying heats had been delayed again because of track problems.

"We could have hunted another hour," Earnhardt said.

"That day was evidently one of the high points of Dale's hunting career," Garner said. "His secretary said he told the story dozens of times in the weeks after the hunt, even getting down on the carpet to demonstrate how we crawled in on the birds."

Garner scuffed his booted toe in the dirt, and a puff of dust blossomed from the dry hillside.

"He was a good man to hunt with," Garner said.

Although Earnhardt was somewhat temperamental on the track — they didn't call him The Intimidator for nothing — the Realtree staff never saw that side of his personality.

"Dale didn't like people using him, his name or his fame," Garner said. "He preferred eating at a drive-through so he wouldn't create a stir or disappoint even one fan. One time, he went to the Rendezvous Restaurant in LaGrange, and before he got out, he'd signed more than 1,200 autographs and caused a traffic jam outside the restaurant. Being in public was very, very difficult for him."

Standing at the spot where Earnhardt killed that last bird, we thought about The Intimidator's public image and how different Dale Earnhardt, dedicated hunter, sounded from Dale Earnhardt, champion driver.

We thought about it until the faint ghost of a gobble floated over the hill in response to Garner's yelps. We headed that way, thoughts of Earnhardt and final turkeys temporarily pushed aside.

We chased that turkey across the farm that morning, criss-crossing Earnhardt's hill several times as we jockeyed to get in position. It was futile, though, as so many hunts are, and we never got close enough. Who knows? It might have been the brother or son of Earnhardt's bird. Or, it might have been the gobbler that got away when Earnhardt's gun jammed.

Somehow, that seemed fitting.

— Jim Spencer, contributing editor for Turkey & Turkey Hunting, *is a confirmed turkey hunting addict from Arkansas.*

CHAPTER 10

Ashley's Wish

Minutes after meeting this green-eyed 10-year-old with the mischievous wink and affectionate nature, I knew she had stolen my heart. A brain tumor, surgery and therapy hadn't dimmed the sparkle in her eyes. When she asked to hunt turkeys with me, I agreed. It was her dream to see a gobbler up close.

■ *TES RANDLE JOLLY*

Everyone has heroes they admire and respect, and whose strength of character enriches their lives.

My parents are my greatest heroes. However, in December 1998, a 10-year-old girl became another hero.

The Bright-Eyed Hunting Partner

I met Ashley Hancock and her family at a Wheelin' Sportsmen of America deer hunt for disabled women. WSA provides outdoor and hunting opportunities for disabled people.

Even at 10, Ashley had killed several deer while hunting with her father. They were close hunting buddies. A brain tumor, subsequent surgery and therapy during Summer 1998 changed the way Ashley hunted, but it didn't diminish her desire.

I was paired with Ashley to assist her during the hunt, and it changed my life. Minutes after meeting this green-eyed child with the mischievous wink and affectionate nature, I knew she had stolen my heart.

Ashley had maintained full use of her left side and limited use of her right arm. However, she had to hunt from a chair. Because Ashley couldn't shoulder a gun, her father, Lou, had built a special gun stand by welding a gun holder to a camera tripod. The holder could be adjusted according to Ashley's directions.

The setup worked, and Ashley shot a fat yearling the first afternoon. Bittersweet joy burned in my soul as she turned, smiled, winked and gave me a thumbs-up. I was humbled by her strength, attitude and determination. She loved to hunt and would not let the battle for her health overshadow her time outdoors.

When Ashley and I hunted deer again in late January, we discussed the upcoming turkey season. By then, we were close hunting buddies. Ashley asked if she could hunt turkeys with me. Her wish was to see a gobbler up close. Without hesitation, I agreed and talked with her parents. Later, we decided my husband, Ron, would join the hunt and attempt to film this special event.

The Road to March

Ashley's family lives in central Florida, so we decided to hunt Florida's spring turkey opener at a private ranch near Ashley's home. Lou and his father-in-law, Buddy Sullivan, planned to scout the area and choose several possible setups. From our home in Alabama, Ron and I drew pictures of how the setup should be to film the hunt. I faxed the drawings to Lou, who was confident he and Buddy would find suitable areas.

Ashley and I talked regularly about our hunt in February and March. She was excited and anxious for March 20. Lou and Ashley spent time shooting turkey targets. He wanted her to be familiar with her gun and know where to aim.

"Miss Tes, I hit the turkey target every time," she said to me on the telephone in early March. "Hurry up and come down so we can go hunting!"

I was anxious, too. Would Ashley remain strong enough to hunt? I prayed daily for two gifts from God: for Ashley to beat cancer and regain her health, and for a gobbler to make her wish come true.

The early morning of March 19, 1999, found Ron and I on the road to Florida. We talked about the next two days. Any turkey hunt can be exhausting, with high-intensity suspense and excitement. We knew this would be that — and more. Ashley's mother, Teri, assured me Ashley was getting lots of rest and looking forward to our arrival.

The family met us at the motel when we arrived.

"Hey, huntin' buddy!" Ashley said from the Suburban.

When I opened the door, she wrapped her arms around my neck in a tight hug.

"Daddy found lots of turkeys," she said, patting my back.

The sparkle in her eyes and the quick smile were still there.

The Eve

After hugs and handshakes, everyone headed for the ranch, where we met Buddy. Although he's a range-hardened cattleman, he unabashedly swept his three granddaughters into his arms, giving them hugs and kisses. Then, Buddy, Lou, Ron and I left Ashley, her mother and her sisters, Nicky and Jamie, to check the setup.

Soon, we put the finishing touches on an oversized ground blind nestled in the low-hanging limbs of an ancient live oak. Buddy and Lou had chosen a perfect setup. The blind, made of live-oak limbs, was on the edge of a live-oak hammock overlooking a pasture. Observers had regularly seen gobblers strutting for feeding hens there before the season. We left a small opening in the blind overlooking the spot where we'd place decoys the next morning.

The morning sun would be at our backs, which was perfect for Ron's camera work. He built a blind about 10 yards behind us, and we left confident everything was in place.

A tour of the ranch revealed several dozen long-bearded Osceolas. Strutters seemed to be everywhere, their backs shimmering iridescent gold and green in the afternoon sun.

I looked at Ron and knew we shared the same thought: This was turkey hunting heaven. Despite Ashley's special needs and having just two days to hunt, our spirits were high.

We returned to the ranch house before sunset, and Ashley met me at the truck. I told her everything was ready for morning. She responded with a strong hug and a hearty, "Yes!"

The Hancock family united to support Ashley's desires. They would wait at the ranch house while we hunted and have a barbecue with all the trimmings after the hunt.

Gobbler Dawn

March 20, 1999, dawned in typical Florida fashion. Dense fog hung like a heavy cloak on the countryside. However, it proved to be an asset because Buddy drove us to the blind. During normal conditions, Lou had to carry Ashley on his back.

In the pre-dawn mist, I noticed our blind had been defoliated during the night. Not one leaf remained on the limbs.

"I guess the cattle in this pasture thought we had set them up a big salad bar," Ron said to Ashley with a laugh.

Ron and Buddy began cutting more limbs for cover. I settled Ashley into her chair and set up the tripod gunstand. Lou set a hen and jake decoy 20 yards from the small opening in the blind. Hopefully, the decoys would increase our chances of calling in a longbeard. If the bird recognized the jake as a threat, he would likely go face-to-face with the decoy.

In minutes, the blind was repaired. Buddy kissed Ashley, wished her luck and drove back to the house to wait with the family.

Gray beards of Spanish moss hung from oak branches as dawn's light gave form to our surroundings. We heard an airboat engine start on a nearby lake. In seconds, the morning's first gobble echoed from a cypress less than 200 yards away. The gobble sounded muffled in the moisture-laden air, but Ashley heard it. She looked at me with her beautiful green eyes and smiled.

"That's the one we're hunting for, isn't it, Miss Tes?" she asked.

Lou and I traded glances. Maybe the bird wouldn't have hens with him. Maybe he'd answer our calling and come to

the decoys. Maybe Ashley's wish to see a turkey up close would come true. I was praying again.

Ron sent a short series of soft, seductive yelps toward the bird, and an eager gobble responded through the fog. Ron signaled that he wouldn't call again till we knew the bird was on the ground.

Here He Comes

The world awakened slowly as the mist gradually rose through the warming air. From every direction, gobblers summoned hens. We heard faint clucks and cackles in the distance, but Ashley sat still, listening intently and whispering an occasional question.

Finally, the tom gobbled from the grassy pasture in front of us. He was on the ground and coming toward us. Ron and I planned to call sparingly, hoping playing hard to get would be the gobbler's undoing. It almost was.

Ron yelped again to the gobbler. Suddenly, there he was — head raised above the weeds, scanning for a hen. He saw the decoys and closed the distance in glorious full strut. After reaching the decoys, the longbeard confronted the jake decoy with aggressive posture.

Ashley's eyes widened with each step the tom took. She was positioned for the shot and asked Lou to push off her gun's safety. The gobbler stood still, engrossed in a stare-down with the jake decoy. We whispered encouragement in labored breaths, and my heart pounded wildly as I sent out silent prayers.

Ashley aimed and fired. My heart sank as the startled gobbler flew. The shot had passed harmlessly over his head.

I feared Ashley would be upset, but I soon learned she didn't perceive missing as failure. She was hunting, and that made her happy.

"Daddy, Miss Tes!" Ashley said. "He was so big and shiny and beautiful! Can we try again?"

Her positive attitude and determination uplifted our spirits. I had wanted Ashley to kill that turkey so much, but I overlooked one thing: She didn't have to kill the tom to realize her wish. She had seen a gobbler up close.

Endless Energy

Buddy arrived soon to pick us up. We spent the next hour at the ranch house laughing, talking about the hunt and photographing Ashley yelping on a box call. We planned for the next day's hunt, when Ashley would return to the ranch after a good rest.

Buddy had found a dry cypress slough where he'd watched several longbeards strut for a flock of hens. Ron believed we

might entice a tom to leave the group if it thought there were two new hens in the area.

The next day, we constructed a blind while Ashley napped at the ranch house. She was up, dressed in camo and ready to hunt by 2 p.m. We prayed for a safe hunt and headed for the blind.

By then, Ashley knew the routine: head-to-toe camo, sit still, listen hard, and watch for movement. And she was serious about it. With a quick glance and low "shh!" she stopped any unnecessary whispering.

As we settled in, Ashley gave Lou directions for some minor adjustments to the gun stand. He then loaded her gun. Ron readied the camera, and the decoys were in place. All we needed was a gobbler.

We listened and watched for a while, but brisk winds made it difficult to hear. Ron urged me to lost-yelp loudly on a box call, and I did. No response. My next series was louder. Lou squeezed my arm and nodded toward the cypress trees in front of us. I looked at Ron, and he smiled an I-heard-it-too grin. Ashley the turkey hunter had pinpointed the sound and was already watching the tree line.

Ron and I used box and mouth calls to imitate several hens. Another gobble responded closer. Ashley focused on the sound and watched intently.

The Wish Comes True

Minutes later, several hens and jakes walked into the opening where we were set up. A gobbler trailed the feeding flock.

"Do you see him, Ashley?" I whispered. "He's following the jakes and hens."

As I whispered, Ashley nodded, and my heart began to pound.

The gobbler followed the hens and jakes, his long beard swinging in the breeze. The birds were approaching quickly, convinced the decoys were real.

Lou looked at me with a prayer in his eyes and began the last-minute positioning of Ashley's gun.

It was like the Osceola gobbler knew what we wanted him to do. He saw the decoys and quickly overtook the flock, gobbling and strutting through the cypress slough. I glanced quickly at Ron, grateful he was preserving the hunt.

As the tom neared, I leaned over to Ashley and helped her tuck the gun into her shoulder and the stock to her cheek. Lou and I whispered encouragement. Ashley had the shotgun aimed toward the decoys, so she'd need little adjustment when the bird arrived.

The gobbler continued to approach the decoys. Ron yelped softly on his mouth call, and the tom returned a

thunderous gobble and strutted closer. His brilliant red, white and blue colors intensified with each step. Finally, the longbeard stopped and confronted the jake decoy.

Ashley was positioned, and she said she was ready.

"You can do it, sugar," Lou whispered as he pushed off the gun's safety.

Ron clucked sharply on his mouth call. The tom raised his head and scanned the brush for a hen.

Time seemed to stand still; the moment is etched in my memory. Seconds ticked by, and the gobbler continued to search for the hen. I knew he might turn and leave immediately. But even if Ashley didn't shoot, her wish had come true again.

Ashley's Gobbler

Distracted by the decoys, the gobbler returned his attention to the jake. Ashley's gaze remained fixed on the magnificent turkey. Holding my breath, I again sent out silent prayers.

Then Ashley squeezed the trigger. Her aim was true.

After the shot, Lou was up, out of the blind and running fast. The Osceola had folded, its feathers shimmering iridescent gold in the afternoon sunlight. Breathing hard, Lou held up the tom for Ashley to see. Pride and love glistened through his brimming eyes.

Tears, smiles and hugs abounded as I helped Ashley to her first turkey. The camera continued to roll, capturing memories that will last forever. Ashley sat with the tom across her lap and stroked the gobbler's shining feathers for several minutes. Then, she looked at her father.

"I love you, Daddy," she said, planting a big kiss on his cheek.

Ron joined us, and we thanked the Lord for the hunt. To say it was emotional is an understatement. I was overwhelmed. It was an unforgettable honor to have been a part of the hunt.

After a lengthy photo session, we rejoined the family, and an inspiring scene of strength, love and deep family commitment unfolded. Everyone gathered to watch the video, anxious to relive the moments with Ashley. Pride shone in her eyes as she related the details.

As Ron and I prepared to leave for home, I knew saying goodbye would be difficult. I knew Ashley's life was in God's hands. We made plans to hunt again in fall. She hugged my neck, gave me a wink and said, "See you next hunting season."

Conclusion

A child is a precious gift, and Ashley was a special child who stole the heart of everyone she met. Sadly, Ron and I returned to Florida in June — not to hunt with Ashley, but to pay our last respects. On June 7, 1999, my friend and hero Ashley Hancock lost her long battle with cancer.

Through it, she never lost her affectionate nature, or her desire to hunt and enjoy the outdoors with family and friends. Her memory serves as an inspiration of strength, love, courage and the spirit of the outdoors to those whose lives she touched.

— Tes Randle Jolly is a longtime turkey hunter, and free-lance writer and photographer from Alabama.

INDEX

ABOUT THE EDITOR

Brian Lovett served as editor of *Turkey & Turkey Hunting* magazine from August 1995 through January 2002.

Lovett, 36, was born and raised in south-central Wisconsin. He attended the University of Wisconsin-Oshkosh, and graduated in Spring 1989 with a degree in journalism. He began his career in November 1988 with the *Oshkosh Northwestern* newspaper, where he served almost four years as the paper's outdoors editor.

In November 1994, Lovett joined Krause Publications to edit *Wisconsin Outdoor Journal*. In 1995, his duties were expanded to include *T&TH*. Along the way, Lovett also edited two books and several specialty magazines, including *Ice-Fishing* and *Realtree Turkey Hunting*. Currently, he is the editor of *Bass Pro Shops' Outdoor World* magazine.

Like many Wisconsinites, Lovett wasn't introduced to turkey hunting until he was in his 20s. He shot his first gobbler in the early 1990s, and has gone on to hunt turkeys in 16 states and Mexico, taking a royal slam and two grand slams. Turkey hunting, waterfowling and upland-bird hunting are Lovett's favorite outdoor activities. He also hunts deer and small game, and fishes for trout, bass and walleyes — after spring turkey season.

Lovett lives in Oshkosh, Wis., with his wife, Jennifer, and black Labrador, Belle.

ABOUT THE PHOTOGRAPHER

Tes Randle Jolly is a free-lance outdoor photographer and writer and active member of the Outdoor Writers Association of America and Southeast Outdoor Press Association. Her work appears in various national and regional outdoor magazines, including Krause Publications, and hunting books. Proud of her American Indian heritage and an avid hunter since childhood, Jolly's outdoor career reflects a deep respect and love of wildlife and the natural world. Her goals are sharing the beauty of nature and passing on the importance of wise conservation of our natural resources through her photography and writing. She lives near Montgomery, Ala., with her husband, Ron.